FORM, SOUND, COLOUR and HEALING

By the same author

HEALING THROUGH COLOUR

FORM, SOUND, COLOUR and HEALING

by Theo Gimbel
DCE, MIACT, MLHRC, NFSH, CERT.ED.

SAFFRON WALDEN
THE C. W. DANIEL COMPANY LIMITED

First Published in Great Britain
by The C. W. Daniel Company Limited
1 Church Path, Saffron Walden,
Essex, CB10 1JP, England

© Theo Gimbel 1987
Reprinted 1990

ISBN 0 85207 186 8

Editorial, Design and Production
in association with Book Production Consultants, Cambridge
Typeset in Palatino by Cambridge Photosetting Services
Printed in Great Britain by St Edmundsbury Press Limited
Bury St Edmunds, Suffolk

This book is printed on recycled paper

This Book is dedicated to the loving memory of
Sir John Langman Bart.
Lady Pamela Langman and the Family

Acknowledgements

I wish to thank especially Angela Wilson who has devoted hour after hour to help me get the content and the English right. Furthermore many of my ex-students, now graduates, who have added so much to the book by posing real questions which I was privileged to answer. In many cases the feedback which they gave me by looking at the draft. In the more technical questions in Chapter V I thank Michael Frye the originator of the Light and Health research council, Clifford Archer, Electronic Design, Robert Wilson for the help with correct terminology on several questions. Pauline Wills who gave vital help to sort out the chapters, Olive Maddock-Dewhurst for all the help with the music. Lastly but not least of all, my very dearest wife Honor who has allowed me to leave her often as a grass widow when I disappeared to do concentrated work on the book, also Sir George Trevelyan, Bt., who has so nobly written the foreword.

Contents

FOREWORD by Sir George Trevelyan — 9

CHAPTER 1 — 11
All that incarnates on this planet is previously pure energy. Between all the galactic spaces, the stars which we can see arise the vase three dimensional patterns which finally incarnate via stone, plant, animal and man into the visible sphere here on earth.

To know these patterns is more and more important for man to maintain his/her own health. In the five regular solids is also manifested the principle of the elements earth, water, fire, air and ether. All are linked to all energies thus, sound colour, light and darkness are found in all things.

CHAPTER 2 — 30
Form is previously sound before it actually 'freezes' into what we call static form. Music is what we hear, but the energies of music are again the principle of how two notes relate to each other. The energy the healing quality is what we cannot hear vibrating between two pitches of sound. The monochord tuning the Pythagorean pitch. The power of music which makes man and all things 'dance' music related to the spine sounds and psychology in man. Music and images. Music and the signs of the Zodiac. Music, the human voice as a force to work on our sexuality. The forces which lie behind names and words. What is the meaning of a name? Positive and negative energies of sound.

CHAPTER 3 — 66
This field of Colour and Patterns – The Aura

The electro-magnetic field (aura); but not to be mixed up with our measurements of magnetism or electricity. The many orders of colour seen in different disciplines. The five octaves of the human spine (five times eight colours ever decreasing in density or increasing in density.)

Spirit – self – superconscious the colours of what we call to be illuminated. The mental ego thinking field yellow which must connect with the emotional–astral–soul blue–this must further communicate through the following systems metabolic–etheris–life, green; and finally reaching into the subconscious physical – sexual being. The ever increasing density of colour throughout the forty vertebrae. Colours by way of prisms their spectrum shifts according to the angles of sunlight in relation to the crystal.

CHAPTER 4 109
Colour Treatment
The bridges which the patient makes according to the spine activities are marked by colour and its complementary colour. When at one point in time a blue appears and an orange also then there is a bridge made and the patient is healing himself. In most cases several bridges turn up whereby the patient communicates with the various areas of mental, emotional, metabolic and physical energies which exchange in a healthy person communications all the time. Where however no complementary colour turns up there we have to use treatment. The assessment of this is the task of the colour therapist.

Communication between these areas naturally depends on the first manifested spirit, superconscious self which is received in our head, the human brain, this comes directly from the cosmic consciousness and awakens in our mental thinking, Ego world from where it must make regular links with all the human person.

CHAPTER 5 138
Instruction and Research Papers

	Page
A threefold approach to a patient involved therapy	138
An outline of three dimensional thinking. Colour, some answers	147
Illumination and colour in infant and primary schools	152
Colour illumination and human sight in relation to health	155
Evidence of colour-influence upon chemical and biological cell structure	163
Observation report on human reactions to coloured illumination	165
Positive changes – a view of how cancer is related to mind and emotions	167
The colour composer in the restoration of mental stability	172
Light as a way to positive health	179
The hexagonal grid of the platonic solids	185
Bibliography	187

Foreword

by Sir George Trevelyan

Theo Gimbel is a pioneer in the field of colour research and colour healing. His inspiration comes from Goethe's theory of colour and its development and application by Rudolf Steiner. It has become clear to many that this field of investigation opens up important possibilities in our age, when a holistic world-view is becoming widely acceptable. In this world-view the thinking of the leading scientists flows together with that of the mystics and with the ancient wisdom traditions. This is perhaps the most significant feature in the spiritual awakening in our time.

Steiner has written: "By experiencing the living element in the flow of colour we come, one might say, out of our own form and share the cosmic life. Colour is the soul of Nature and the whole cosmos, and by experiencing the life of colour we participate in this soul".

It becomes clear that Colour Therapy is of great significance in the whole wide field of Complementary Medicine and Healing. Yet what are the qualifications that make a Colour Therapist? What is the training necessary to attain such qualifications? This is a new field and it becomes necessary to explore and to establish some way of measuring and assessing the standard of skill and proficiency needed to work as a Colour Therapist

Theo Gimbel, in his remarkable centre in Brook House, Avening, has pioneered this work and is offering training course, to those who wish to enter this field. It has been an outstanding achievement, combining years of patient, scientific investigation with artistic sensitivity and creative craftsmanship. In this relatively new field, Brook House is able to offer a standard for training and a qualification for those who have gone through it.

In this book Theo Gimbel brings together his findings and demonstrates their practical applications. His work is achieving international recognition and will now be carried forward by those who have won qualification in this form of Colour Therapy offered at Brook House.

The vision is very wide and truly includes the spiritual nature of man and the universe. Art and Science are linked, and the most practical knowledge of the deeper nature of the human being is given to us.

This book has much of interest for the layman who wants to understand the living nature of colour. For those who wish to work in this field it will be essential reading. The wisdom in these pages represents a life devoted to a wonderful and fascinating field of exploration. May it achieve the success and recognition that it truly deserves.

Chapter 1

Colour Forms and Rhythms

As we become aware of our environment, the observing man must ask many questions: how is it that we can find in all the manifested earth crystals, plants, animals and man always the blue prints which seems not only to be within but also seems to give the form principles in which it appears?

If there is a structure within the visible structure, is there not also an outer infinitely large structure which interrelates to all our visible world.

Healing Through Colour (p. 172–173) ends with two images, and it is a good continuation to look at these wonderful forms. Out there in the galactic space is a structure by way of the starry heavens. Each star "looks" at all the others using a beam of light which inter-communicates.

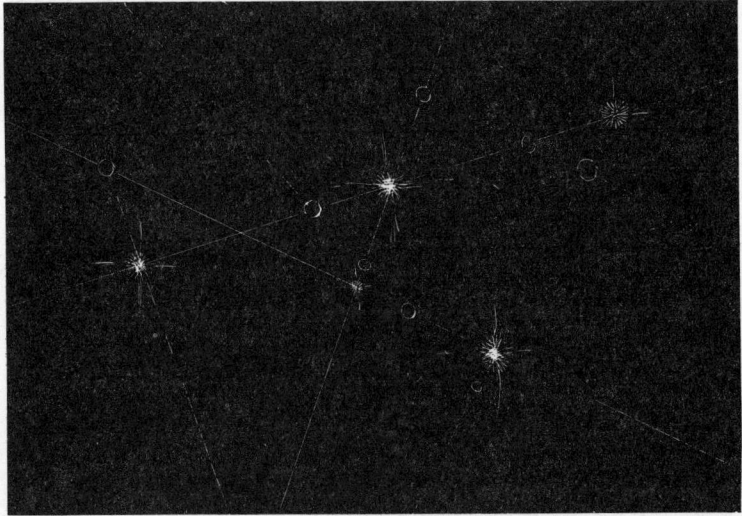

Fig 1.1

Fig 1.2

All possible structures are there, those we have already recognised and such which are still to be discovered. Each energy point or star has two principle radiations, one of linear patterns centre to infinity in straight beams of light. The other in spherical patterns like spheres surrounding all other spheres from the nucleous tiny sphere (too small to see) to the vast spheres which hold all galaxies, (too vast to see) because of the spherical shape of the earth the opportunity arises for the platonic solids to crystalise. The sphere is the non-form.

The laws which are penetrating down into this earth sphere create the five main directives, and the laws are the will of God to bring consciousness to earth.

But again, within this visible structure of the constellations is also contained the invisible structures amongst which are black holes where we must suspect that, because of the void space, light travels faster than light and thereby there is total darkness which causes what is known as the geometric warp. Space becomes time, and time becomes space.

The reason why the structures are so significant is that specifically the cube, or hexahedral shape, is so very important for this earth. The three dimensional form is basically our orientation and therefore a law of this planet on which we live. It has also a very valuable reference at the very end of the New

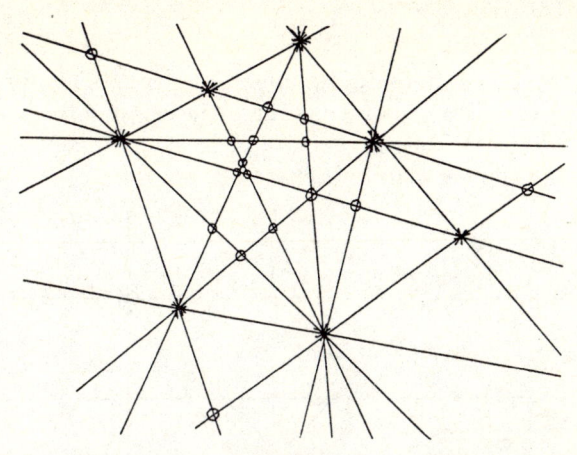

Fig. 1.3 The principle of the visible stars creating the void places such as black holes Stars = *bl.H. = 0

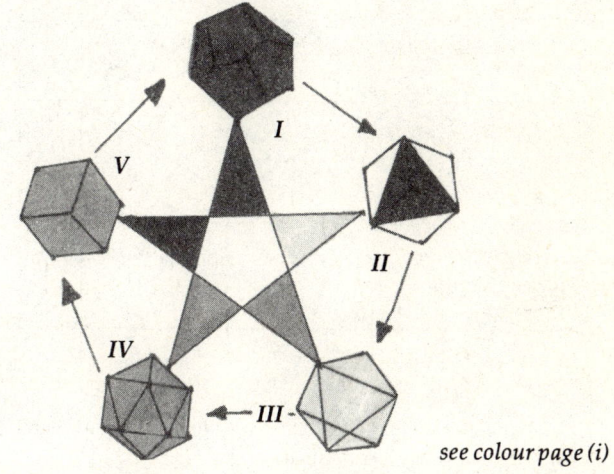

Fig 1.4 The five octaves of the human spine hold the following energies:
I God being
   Spirit, Higher Self, superconscious, (Head, extended vertebra, according to Rudolf Steiner)
II Man
   Ego, thinking mentality, intellect. (Cervical I, including Thorasic I)
III Animal
   Astral, emotional self, soul feeling. (Thorasic 2–10)
IV Plant
   Etheric – physical. Not to be confused with the cosmic ether, but a lower part of this. Life energy, metabolic. (Thorasic II – lumbar 5)
V Mineral
   Physical, sexuality, subconscious (Sacrum in eight parts)

Form, Sound, Colour and Healing

Testament, the Book of Revelations, Chapter 21. The number 12 occurs again. The six outer (square) faces, and the six inner (triangular) faces. The number 12 is of great significance for a real healing concept of man to be based upon.

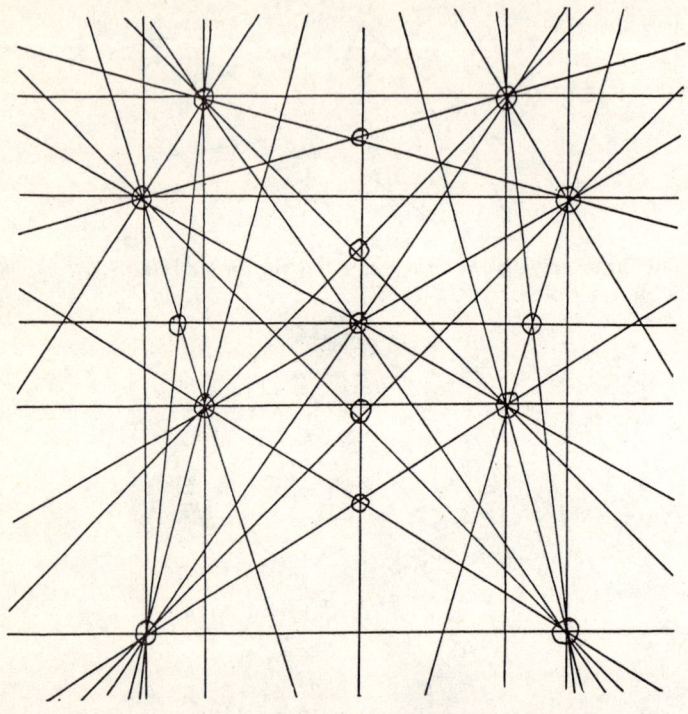

Fig 1.5 Revelation, Chapter 21 verses 10 to 22. Carefully read will show the Hexahedron as being the new city.

Fig 1.6 The internal faces of the cube, Hexahedron.

Colour Forms and Rhythms

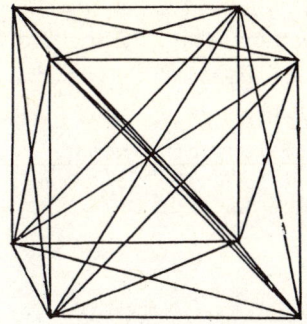

Fig 1.7 Stage 1

2 diagonals on each of 6 faces but each diagonal represents both flow and counter-flow = 24 energy patterns. Stage I all possible diagonals are shown. Into this we can now introduce the next stage II pattern.

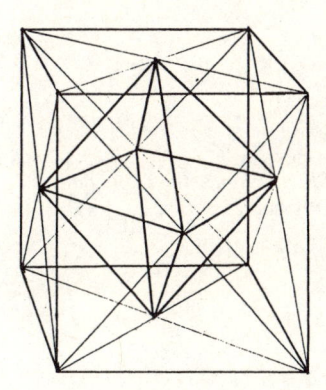

Fig 1.8 Stage II

The dual of the hexahedron becomes the interior pattern. Stage II* is just an offset pattern to show stage II more clearly.

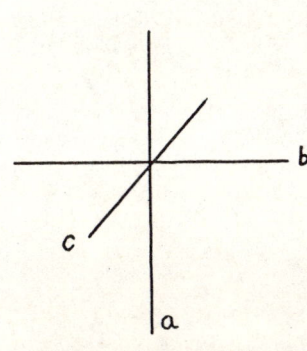

*Fig 1.9 Stage II**

This stage II* can now accept the most important three dimensional orientation for man on this earth.

(a) the vertical (red)
(b) the horizontal (blue)
(c) the transitional (yellow)

We can now say: The vertical must be the most conscious state of being upright, thus the red colour supports this direction. The horizontal balance of life, the blue colour seems to fit this best; and the last of the three is the transitional, the path in the yellow colour.

When we look at many of the symbols around us, we find the

15

most simple structure is the cross. The celtic cross adds the spheric (circle) indication. Today we must also add the 3rd Dimension (red, blue, yellow).

Fig 1.10 Red

Now we have what is called in Geometry the door plane, red, which is the plane that indicates: I see.

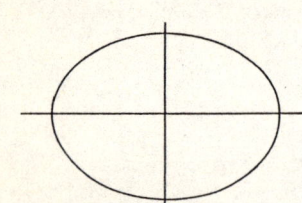

Fig 1.11 Blue

The second of these planes, the table plane is blue, it in turn signifies: I serve.

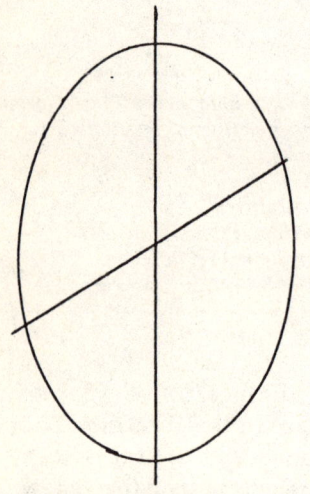

Fig 1.12 Yellow

The third plane, the wheel plane is taken from this wholeness as a trinity meaning, I go.

Now we can say: I see, I serve, I go. This all placed together creates the healing structure of the 3 Dimensional sphere of

Colour Forms and Rhythms

orientation or healing of Form (directions) and colours, (the three primary colours). Red is always the active colour, blue the passive (serving) colour and yellow the leading on or spiritual light we can follow.

Fig. 1.13

see colour page (ii)

Fig. 1.14 The three dimensional cross.

We can lift ourselves into this state of consciousness by way of the seven steps raising ourselves through our own instrument, the body, through the seven steps up into this new awareness;

17

Form, Sound, Colour and Healing

Fig. 1.15 see colour page (ii)

hence the ever evolving spiral steps indicating the major glands. From below making its way upwards following through from the sacral, adrenals, solar plexus, heart, throat, pituitary to the pineal.

Gazing into the myriad of stars at night we become aware that we are just one, maybe tiny orb in our galaxy. This means that there are countless bodies held in an order which to most of us seems to be random, even chaotic.

Fig. 1.17

Colour Forms and Rhythms

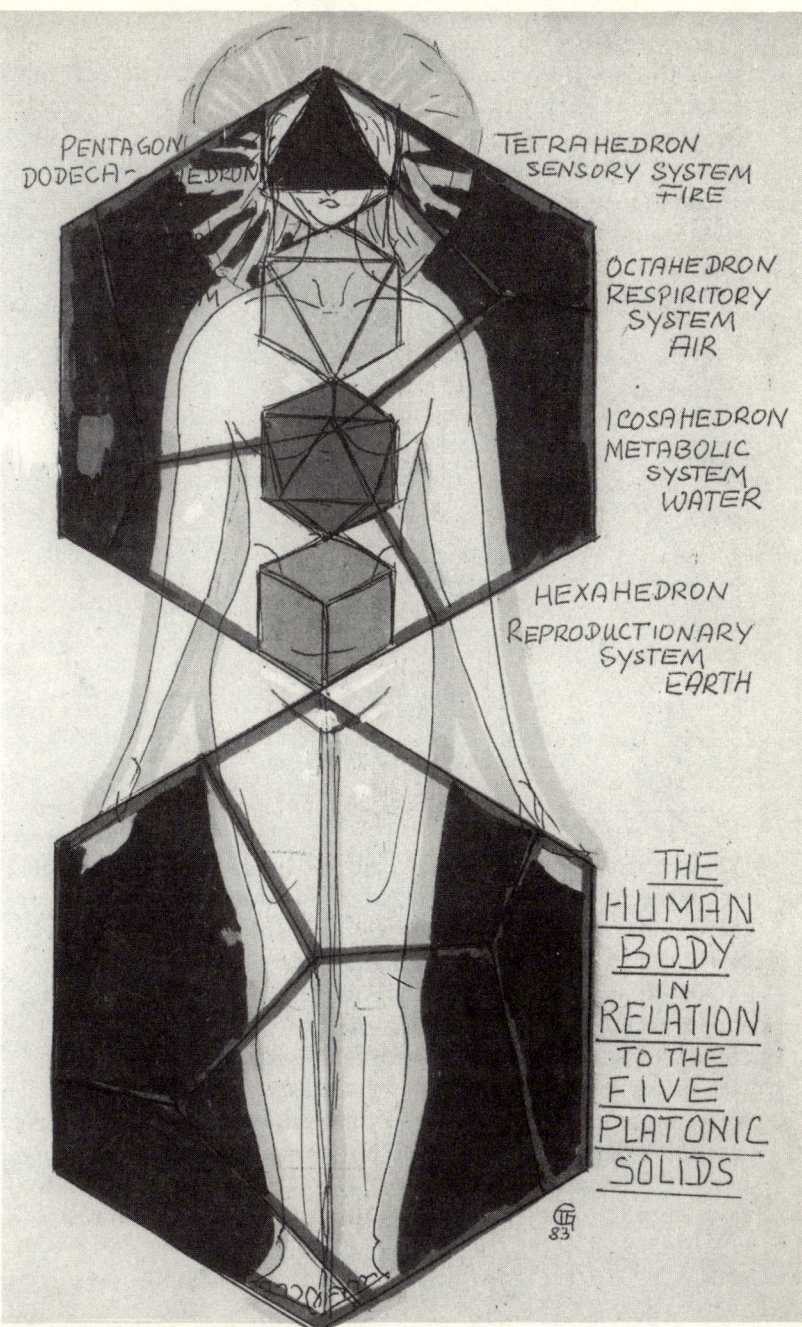

Fig. 1.16. See colour page (iii)

Form, Sound, Colour and Healing

Each star has a magnetic and antimagnetic energy. It can also be said that the magnetic energy is gravity whereas the antimagnetic energy is that energy which Sir Isaac Newton took seventeen years to research but could not find. If we talk, however, about the energy which lies around all visible objects, we can more and more call this radiation, or the etheric energy.

This radiation has two main forms: One linear from the centre into affinity; the other spherical.

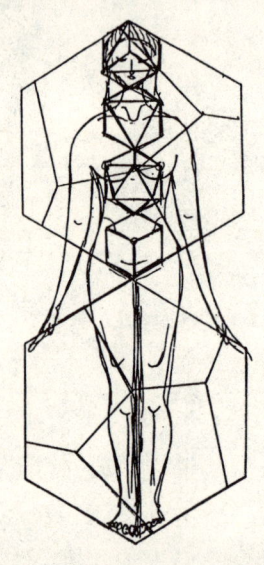

Fig. 1.18

Selecting from the infinite patterns those which ultimately create the five Platonic solids, we can suddenly recognise that there is also the human form standing behind, between, inside or around it. The image of God and we are made in this image.

Our whole body composed of Fire, Air, Water and Earth being shot through with the etheric energy of life across. Also, of course, these life forces are within and around all that is alive;* (see pages 28–38, *Healing Through Colour*). Just imagine that all forces are within all forces, and all forces are around all that is, was and will be. The Universe is breathing, singing and dancing because of, and on behalf of God, who is love, and love that we now learn to give, in unlimited and undemanded quantity.

*The C. W. Daniel Co. Ltd. Theo Gimbel 1980 ISBN 85207 1566

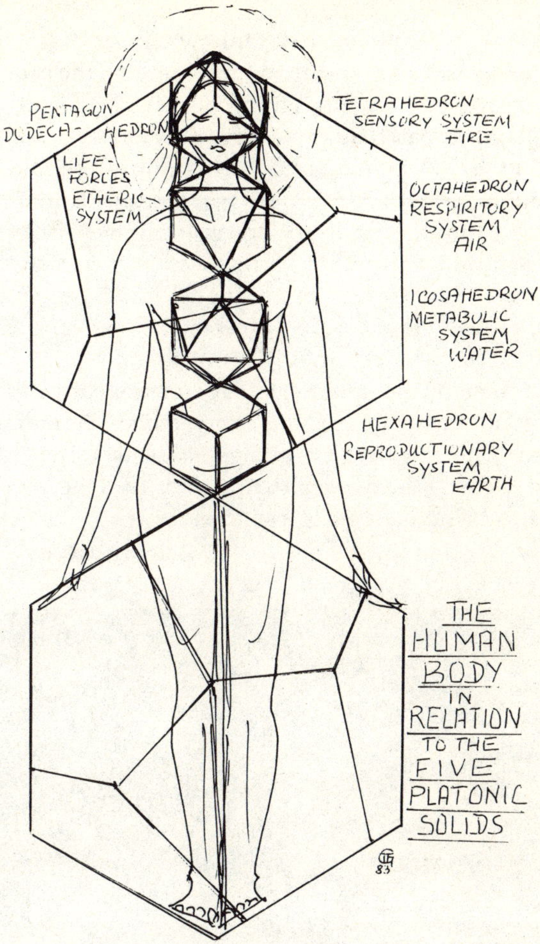
PENTAGON DODECA- HEDRON
LIFE-FORCES ETHERIC SYSTEM
TETRAHEDRON SENSORY SYSTEM FIRE
OCTAHEDRON RESPIRITORY SYSTEM AIR
ICOSAHEDRON METABOLIC SYSTEM WATER
HEXAHEDRON REPRODUCTIONARY SYSTEM EARTH
THE HUMAN BODY IN RELATION TO THE FIVE PLATONIC SOLIDS
83

Fig. 1.19

Blue mixed with yellow = green
Yellow mixed with red = orange

We add to this

Violet mixed with red = magenta
Turquoise with violet = blue

When using light and not pigment (in the subtractive colour range).

Also, here we recognise again the duality experience. This short appraisal into the colours is also applicable to forms, to all

Form, Sound, Colour and Healing

the physical environment. Only when we dissolve the physical can we reach the one-state which contains the duality within but not in space or time in an infinity-eternity state.

All our research ought to be carried out on every level (a) form (b) colour (c) mathematical, etc. and all should be looked at through the aspects of these many ways. Colour seen through form, form through colour; nothing is disconnected, all is interwoven. The eternal, infinite state is present but cannot be weighed, measured or counted with our rough physical apparatus where it always escapes the scientific statistical work. That does not mean that it is not there.

Because of the spherical shape of the earth, the opportunity arose for the Platonic solids to crystalise. The sphere is the none-Form. The laws which are penetrating down into this earth sphere create the five main directives, and the laws are the will of God to bring consciousness to earth.

Our body is created in two ways; the spiritual, superconscious

Fig. 1.20. See colour page (iv)

Colour Forms and Rhythms

or higher self which uses the soul, and the astral which communicates with matter in the form of the earth energies of air, fire and water. Therefore the human being is the result of the co-operation between heaven (the spiritual world) and the manifested planet earth (the physical world).

The way in which this is being done is that, like all visible matter, the God Spirit brings harmony, rhythm and form into this interplay between the forces of earth and those of the Spirit. And, not surprisingly, these forms are the now well-known five major forms, the Platonic Solids. Minerals, plants, animals and humans are incarnating through these five regular solids. The spiritual etheric energies penetrate into the earthly etheric life forces and create in this communication the seeds which are the beginning of all visible things.

These seeds are like the finest, most delicate filters through which is pouring the forces of form, sound, colour, light and darkness, selecting such balances which are to become us, or any of the visible Kingdoms around us.

Our air body is created by way of taking the yellow octahedron form and building our respiratory system. The fire (warmth) body used the red Tetrahedron, the water body is expressed through the blue Icosahedron and the earth (mineral) body through the green Hexahedron. All these four elements are penetrated by the ether – life forces which come in the form of the Pentagon – dodegahedron.

Out of the darkness God spoke: Let there be light, and by this light came the inner and the outer sense of sight. Thus we can form images and even in the absence of any we can recall through the inner sight any of the forms we wish to remember. Our health body can greatly be helped if we can use this image making in the following way.

When we are cold we can imagine a luminous red Tetrahedron (the element of fire) shining with warmth into our mind. From there let it go to any place and direct it to my hands which could be cold, my feet or any part, or indeed the whole of myself, and strongly making the picture and then offer gratitude to the element of fire I will be warm, comfortably so, not hot which becomes too much.

When my respiratory (breathing system), is upset, not doing as well as it should, then I can use the octahedron yellow, very luminous, again and imagine this to direct my breathing. If there is too much air in my metabolic system I can see this yellow octahedroninal there, see it get smaller and smaller because it is air that has gone into the wrong place. You can breath not only with your lungs, through your nose but also through any part of you. Stretch out your hands and let them breath with a little practise you learn to breath anywhere. As the body of air represents the sense of hearing, the octahedron can be used in visualisation to improve this sense. Again you may like to direct this sound perception to your back instead of only to your ears. Every cell has all ourselves as a potential so why not use it.

When we wish to be in better harmony with the element of water then let us use the Icosahedron, the shining blue, and ask for the correct water energies to be used in our body. Equally we need at times, to have the balance of this earth, the solidity, to the right degree, and for this we can use the hexahedron to give us the right crystaline structures, the green colour of manifestation.

Lastly, we must remember that all these four bodies of the sacred Geometry are originally created out of the energies of the spiritual – cosmic ether-world, and this etheric spiritual energy is available in all the other four, as well as having its own form. The most perfect harmony body is made from the twelve pentagons which conduct the etheric energies into all bio-chemical structures, even the crystals are full of this life energy. Both in the cells, the atom, as also in the galactic space. The physics of the very large are the blue print for the physics of the very small and all forms, colours, sounds, light and darkness are inter-communicating omnipresent and, dancing–singing–shining–touching–scent producing nourishment for us to be well.

Again, we have to accept the complexity of our environment and state: as above, so below, as within, so without.

One more version of the hexahedron is the incredible rose pattern of this 3D body. (*see Fig. I (II)*) very clearly created as the 3D Cross, a symbol of orientation and healing.

The two foldness of the linear (radial) pattern being complemented by the spheric (global) pattern. The connections in these structures are quite astounding. Taking the principles which lie behind all that, what becomes manifested into the world which man can weigh, measure and count, we arrive at the recognition

Colour Forms and Rhythms

that out of this one state, the duality state comes into the earth. Since it comes out of the one-state it wants to unite again. The purpose is always to create a third which aspires to unite to the original one-state, this is however, in the physical, not possible. Out of this challenge arises the search for the eternal, which leads ultimately back to the one-state; but it will always remain a spiral and not a return to its absolute origin. In the pure light experiments we come to realise that we have colour and complementary colour, that two colours mixed and blended create a third colour. In pigment colours, this is not as pure as it is in light colours. Pigment holds too much (impure) matter. Goethe* in his book written in 1810, *ZUR Farben-Lehre*, translated the title is *Towards a teaching of Colour* works with this phenomena of colour in a most outstanding way he comes to colour experiences (which very well complement Sir Isaac Newton's work), red mixed with blue makes the third colour violet.

Fig. 1.21. See colour page (iv)

*Johann Wolfgang von 1749–1832

Hygeia The Greek goddess of healing belongs to one of those elevated being who in fact did not physically incarnate during this earth existence. Hygeia passed through the stages of a human-life initiation, or a comparable experience, on a planet which preceded this earth and its physical life as we know it today. She experienced this contraction into matter, suffered the limitations and the dis-ease as we do today long before our planet called upon the human being to undergo this life which entails the weight, the measure and the time-space-experience. Thus Hygeia was well prepared, well attuned to know what we ourselves are experiencing today. We can take from such thoughts naturally the great comfort, that we shall inherit such states which are her own now.

Hygeia-Elohim is a very close companion to the Christ-Elohim both sharing the total consciousness state, which is for us as yet too powerful to endure. These beings are all-conscious, all-feeling, all-hearing, seeing all that all beings human, below human and above human are. In the total awareness nothing is hidden. Therefore such highly elevated beings can fully understand, absolutely experience what any creature is undergoing now, has been and will be. They live beyond space and time; there is only a complete presence, nothing less or more is possible, because there is the omnipresent of the Holy Trinity.

Hygeia has however taken upon herself the important task, to help the human race to go successfully through the learning of how to keep well, and steer man to understand his growing mastery over all matters that finally become complete harmony and balance. She gazed upon our state with objective, construction compassion. She is not sorry, nor is she pleased, she is! She responds to our calls, but will not act unless approached by us.

The Patterns of Recovery. On the way to a better health.

The general thinking by and large accepts that we travel a journey from A to B; yes and no, we do and we do not. Thus let us assume that we do. We also have built into our system the ambition that we should do better, reach higher etc. Thus we add to this journey another perspective.

```
A ─────────────────────── B
                         B1
A ─────────────────────── B
```

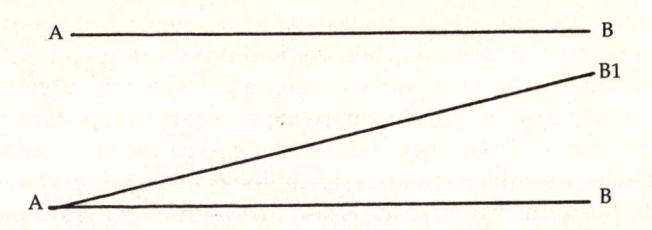

This new aspect is again true at the same time not true. If we study the patterns of our life we can see that there are ups and downs. These we can learn to control. Our wish to be happy and make progress produces an extra high, thus we can see that potentially we are rising at an even steeper angle than we would normally take.

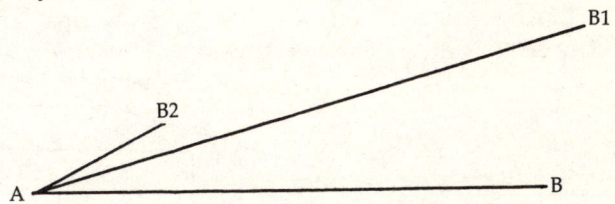

```
                              B1
         B2
A ─────────────────────── B
```

However, if we are to keep control of this growth we must accept that an accelerated progress has to be anchored in order to be meaningful for our own progress. This anchoring must take into account our whole person in time and space. So, we arrive at our next part of the journey with both a present and a past to add to our future. Many people do not allow that we can, to a greater and ever increasing amount, become in charge of this future; understanding it however is the first step to becoming the conductor.

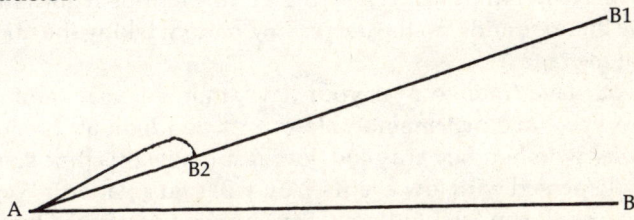

```
                              B1
          B2
A ─────────────────────── B
```

However it is not enough only to grow up, we must also grow deeper, and this can involve 'pain'. Pain is the teacher and joy is the energy. Do not however make pain an issue of misery but ask how to learn from it for when we will not have to endure this pain. So we let our experiences make a link with our past. Now we can see that in time and space we are creating a pattern. The time factor is as follows: take the measure of hours and by research, trial and error we arrive at the time factor of 40 hours. Underlying this pattern of 40 is also the rhythms of the Fibonacci series of harmonic development. Thus when we have started any special part of our journey after one day and night plus 2 or 3 hours we have to allow a 'relapse', this permits us to deepen the newly absorbed experience. Thus for a day and an hour or two we deepen, i.e. link what we now know to all our past experiences. From this point we can then take off and undertake through this insight our next part of the journey.

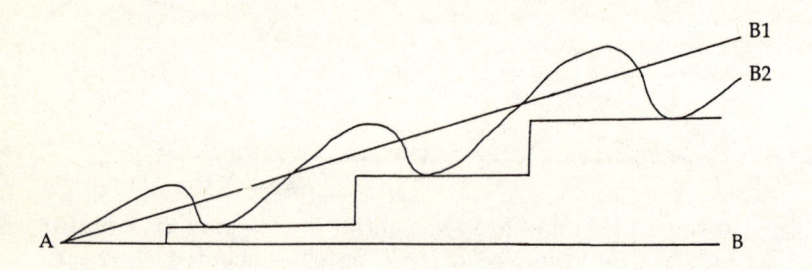

Each time we allow this to happen we can say that the pain is less and less necessary as we learn to control our own inner self and conduct meaningfully the programme of our life.

No one trough is as low as the previous one but be more significant to us. Look at the ocean and see how the waves behave every 14th is a specially high one and thus it goes into 7 on the increase and 7 on the decreasing pattern taking the middle as the average.

If you have time go over your days, months, years and find where you have met memorable events and look at them and consider whether they are good, joyful and how this time span is inter-dispersed with low events. You will find a pattern. We can always, by the understanding of this, become comforted that the plan is meaningful if not always just for fun only. But there is a plan, one which you can make and one which happens if you do not make one. By making a plan you can become more and more the master of your events and knowing the growth pattern you can now have a say in what is to come, or better to happen to you.

All these events which show in their development an underlying pattern which is three (3) can be said to hold an awakening pattern within. Thus 3, 6 or 9 and so forth are always figures which must be looked at with this kind of view.

Also we can observe the 'step' development and its energy (rise).

Chapter 2

Sound, Words, and Music in support of Colour Therapy

Sound is the centre, the originator of form and form is the resounding "echo". There are as many different violin sounds as there are violins; as many different colours of voices as there are people.

An instrument being built cannot on its own start to play unless it is *moved* to play. Ultimately even the human being is moved to speak or sing. Light was created that shines into darkness and light moves, and thereby creates sound. A candle shines in its colour and by its coloured light creates a silent sound this sound is not unheard as it creates the form of the light.

One sound sounded is a "reminder". One sound in pitch is "a path". Two sounds in harmony create form and call for a third energy. A triad chord creates "a state".

What is enclosed between three becomes a realm and establishes sufficient security that justifies it in staying and being. A chord in healing can be said to be an anchor; it represents three dimensions.

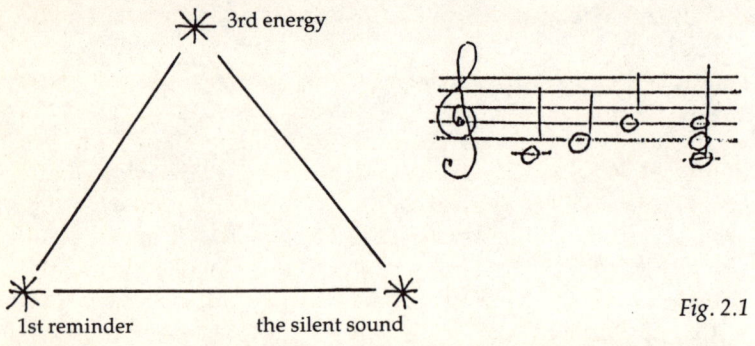

Fig. 2.1

The two main trends in disease are the static in the extreme and the over mobile. In the static is held fast that which should flow and in the mobile is flowing that which should be static. There seems to be today a great amount of disease that stems from the static, the holding on to what should be fluid. The other trend seems to be in the minority. Man must be the balance between the two. Sound becomes meaningful when there appears the state of the chord that lends security to the flow of a path, which is melody. In reality we should not hold anything at all. We should, like the sound, move on from state of being to state of being, i.e. one key to another. To return to the home key, the one that we started with, is only a reminder that we have moved and come through a progression. After several sounds and chords, returning to the home key is like seeing it from above, a step higher, and on that step it is now to be secured by a new concept of further experience. Thus a patient is moved into this new level by the experience of the flow of music; in the final "home key" they find the memory of what has gone before.

Lower sounds are solemn and stand as a foundation; higher ones are joyful and lead upwards. As much as sounds create, they can also kill. *Sound in healing can thus be used to set into flow that which has become static. Intervals, too can be used to set into flow what has become static. The intervals which are used are significant, and we must be aware that much checking must be done to find the intervals which lead to healing in each individual being. Hygeia Studios research into healing sound.

There is a scale of sound in each human spine which can bring us to an awareness of where to go to find what we need to know for the healing of an individual. Each interval has healing qualities of its own. The human spine is constructed by the vertebrae in such a fashion that the concepts of music can be fond in it (See Fig. II.2). Every human being has an imperfect spine and the vertebrae reflect the total health pattern of each person, each of us is playing with the equilibrium to maintain the health of the whole body. The points which register in the course of 24 hours are mostly not disease but serve the adjustment of life. This life adjustment is both physical, emotional and mental. Some of the vertebrae register either frequently or permanently in which case we do have to accept that this is a chosen problem or task for this life time.

There is very rarely only one vertebrae "out of tune" in the spine. These intervals are now used by incorporating them in a

Form, Sound, Colour and Healing

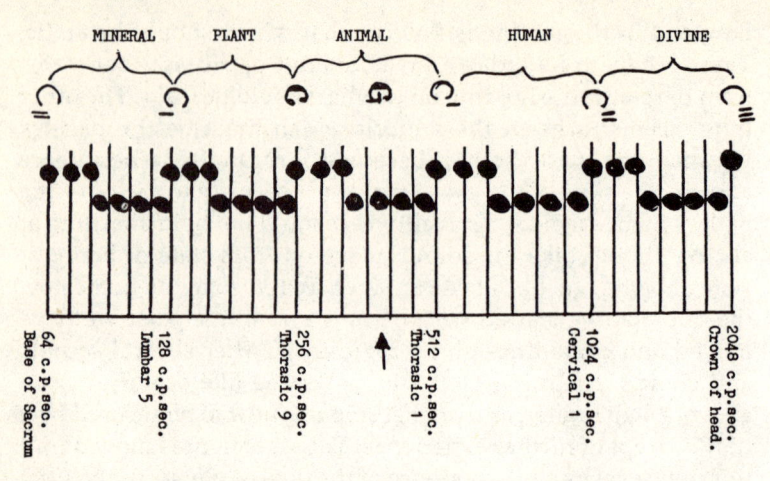

[Figure 2.2: A diagram showing a musical scale spanning MINERAL, PLANT, ANIMAL, HUMAN, DIVINE ranges, with frequencies labeled: 64 c.p.sec. Base of Sacrum; 128 c.p.sec. Lumbar 5; 256 c.p.sec. Thoracic 9; 512 c.p.sec. Thoracic 1; 1024 c.p.sec. Cervical 1; 2048 c.p.sec. Crown of head.]

Fig. 2.2

sequence of sounds (melody) which will be supported by chords. (A guitar is an ideal instrument for this purpose).

The points of imbalance make up a group of intervals which form the basis of the healing music for each individual patient.

We still have great obstacles to overcome before we can use recorded sound as healing sound. Our own experiences here is that the true harmonics must be used. On the question of pitch in healing sound, middle C should be taken to read 256 c. p sec, this is eight vibrations lower than today's concert pitch. This pitch coincides with the sound of the human bone forms.

Total distortion of harmonics will always occur in present recordings. While listening to recorded sound we are aware of the frequencies, but not aware that the true understanding and meaning of the music is only revealed to us because we are continually correcting subconsciously what is distorted. Thus if we wish the finer bodies of man to be affected by true sound we must use live sound, even at the cost of being far from perfect or beautiful compared with a seemingly "perfect" recording.

Healing in the temples was given together with the sounds that issued from the priests, choruses, etc. After all, when all is said and done, the human voice is as complete an instrument as we can wish for. All instruments are only an aspect of total sound. In the human voice we can come closest to what is known as the harmony of the spheres.

Sound, Words, and Music in support of Colour Therapy

To each sign of the zodiac is allocated two of the twenty-four keys of western music. In accordance witlh the work of Rudolf Steiner we can see the signs of the zodiac in a new light. In fact, not really fixing the key but standing between the keys. Thus the sign of Libra, for example, is standing on the threshold between B major/A♭ minor and F major/E♭ minor. In this way there is a truly living interval that signifies each sign.

The planets are then moving melody and can be said to represent the single tones, but as these move through the signs they create chords and discords, both necessary to each other as darkness is to light. In this way, we can see how there is a major and a minor sound influencing human health through the zodiac. There are still big tasks ahead. In today's work we must be aware that individuals can only truly help if they are also servants of a group, and learn to allocate and co-operate in the work of man. Consciousness can only be be found if we all very deeply acknowledge that we attain self-knowledge through our fellow men, otherwise we are not aware. Gratitude, and above all, LOVE – that must become the gift man offers as his contribution to the world.

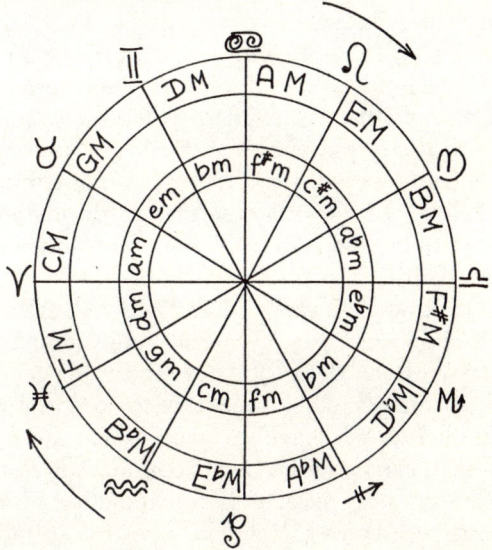

Fig. 2.3 Herman Beckh (Prof.): "Vom Geistigen Wesen der Tonarten" (about the spiritual significance of the keys) (Plate 3) Verlag Preuss + Junger Breslau. 1932.

The experience of sound is a continual teaching to man. In this education is incorporated the evolution and the rhythms of progress.

The experience of sound can come to man's consciousness only because sound appears in rhythms and not as an unbroken continuous tone. Furthermore, the pitch of this sound varies and in fact uses shorter or longer intervals to create melodies by which his soul is stirred. Such melodies can be compared with walking – sometimes taking long steps, sometimes short steps. Over the whole there rises the ebb and flow of breathing; with this action of breathing we hold health and harmony in our being.

Sound on the physical plane, is very much a poor echo when compared with some higher experience of sound, sometimes referred to as the music of the spheres. When we extend our awareness levels we become able to hear the sounds that the celestial bodies create in their orbits. When this music is heard it is not limited by beginning or ending; such sound is continuous; it is the change of harmonies created by the moving of planets through the fixed star system, the Zodiac.

Each sign of the Zodiac has two aspects of sound combinations. It may be said that a sign carries on the one hand the G major chord, and holds as a balance the E minor triad (chord). A planet that enters into the orbit of this sound complex will change the original experience and challenge its complacency.

We must not, however, look at this phenomenon with our modern logical minds; we must use real intuition and imagination, thus breaking through into another dimension where physical laws cannot apply.

The twentyfour keys, if really considered well are a spiral and not a circle, however this in earth bound music becomes impossible to work out. Before Johann Sebastian Bach the tuning of musical instruments was still closer to the original concepts of spheric music. But we have to progress and the result is consciousness. It can again be said: To go back is not right, but by a spiritual appraisal we can only conclude that a future music can be free again and on a higher level obey the spiral form once more.

We will become aware that there we are in the presence of a universal teaching which has no equal here, in the physical

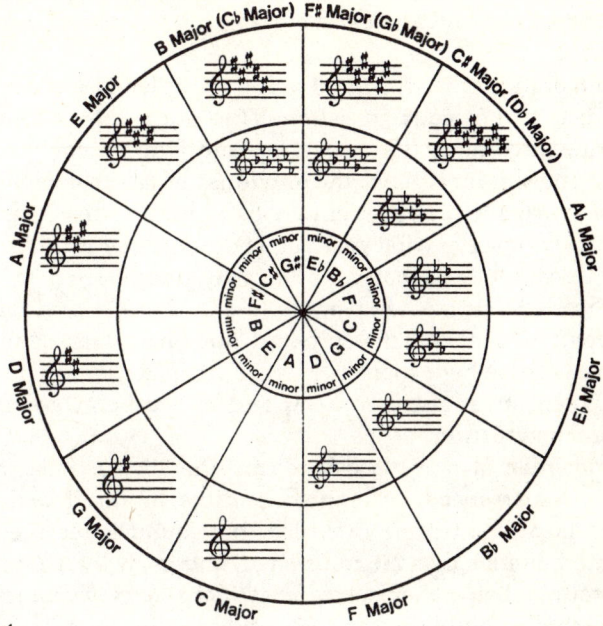

Sound, Words, and Music in support of Colour Therapy

Fig. 2.4

realm. We must make a break-through in our minds to cross lateral thinking. With this new mental awareness we can experience these more subtle vibrations which are the properties of the Planets as individual sounds, and the harmony vibration of a certain key or chord. These harmonies, held by a given sign of the Zodiac, are like the personality of a mother holding the pulsating life and prepared to be visited by a Planet, a father, who will change the expectant state into a pregnant state out of which is born a new harmony, creating thus a new state of the "mother".

There are twelve signs, hence twelve mothers, each being a unique constellation, and by this constellation is determined the character of that mother. We know that in our solar system we count eleven planets; these father principles have the power to give life to each of these mother principles as they visit these constellations.

We must try and see how, in all this movement of the stars, there is no alpha and no omega, but alpha and omega are places of consciousness, nodes to hold, in order that man can mark the evolution of life – awareness – metamorphosis – and grasp the inversions.

A sign of the zodiac is a fixed point which lends security for a movement to be made in safety. This point then allows the venturing into a new view, aspect or stage. Only when there then is fixed a new point equal to the previous one can that which was fixed move again. (The reader may like to walk a few steps and very clearly observe what each leg is doing stage by stage; one has to remain still so that the other may progress.)

By these changes, when planets enter a sign a new singing is developed which has never been, nor shall ever again, be possible. And where there is a voice to speak, to sing and to create, there must also be an ear and eye to be aware of this grandeur in creation.

Sound must at one place fade into the silence as it travels beyond its own speed, becoming inaudible. In this place there is thereby created a temple in which that sound is received and venerated. Beings live, are nourished, and grow by listening to these sounds being themselves in a total silence. Furthermore, what is there, shining out in light and creating the numberless constellations, is seen in these temples because in the Light there is nourishment, thus there is total darkness – Light has gone beyond its own speed. So, out of sound and light grows silence and darkness as a necessity to creation. These places seem to be the complementary universe completing the visible constellations by being the invisible counterparts. One day there will be a new star shining where there is now a temple of silence and darkness, or can we say a womb in the process of creation.

What such temples are like is hard to describe. One great point that must be made is, that we must look into these temples with the deepest feeling of clear awe and wonder; a love that has no measure; an angelic approach that is hard to create for a moment, let alone to hold in time and space.

Yet such thoughts and concepts must begin to grow, and though as yet unspoken, there must arise in our deepest feeling the knowledge that a bridge will be built for the time that will come. The time that is, that was, that will be, when we grow nearer to the celestial orbs and become greater beings, with deeper roots that may grow into that prepared field of the spirit.

In other words, we will need to understand that beyond both speed of sound and light dwell the mysterious silences – the unfathomable darkness – which creates new foundations for worlds, without end.

Earth music is often full of sounds that are too close together and leave little or no space for the harmonies or overtones to ring through.

A sound needs space to experience around itself the attributes of its own harmonies. We should be careful to write music with this in mind; we should be careful not to fill all the possible places in a chord, but work more with extended chords. Good examples are well-written four part compositions such as string quartets and four voice songs.

Creating an experience of distance between two sound enhances the space between, or the unheard sound which with experience, will manifest as sound in our consciousness. We should know that the measure of sound has a very deep root in the proportions of sacred geometry. Our research in this area can start with a monochord.

Real experiences are made when we use this instrument in the following way:

Monochord tuning
All these sounds are only approximate, as the modern piano does not fall within the correct intervals of the monochord.

The Monochord is tuned to $G_{\prime\prime\prime}$ (two G below middle C.) The string is 1000 mm long.

$1/10 = A''$ on the short part of the string and $1/90 = A_{\prime\prime}$ and as follows on:

*1/5 1/20 = B'	1/80 = $B_{\prime\prime}$
*1/4 1/25 = G'	1/75 = $C_{\prime}$
1/30 = E'	1/70 = $C_{\prime}\sharp$
*1/3 1/3.333 ... = D'	1/66.666 ... = $D_{\prime}$
1/40 = B'	1/60 = $E_{\prime}$
1/50 = G'	

* The 3–4–5 fractions make up the E minor chord which is the basic tuning of the Guitar.

Form, Sound, Colour and Healing

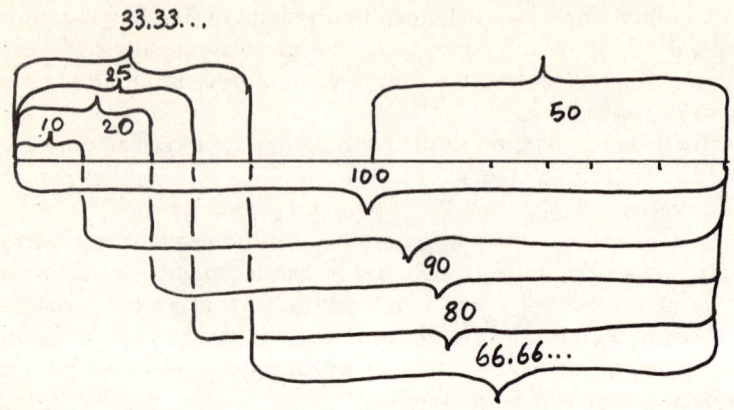

Fig. 2.5

We must not, however, experiment in this way out of curiosity; we must consciously consider what use these experiments hold for humanity. Research and experiment are only meaningful if we incorporate them into our physical kingdom, right down to the very mineral upon which we stand. All is actually sound captured in matter, very little of which is heard by the human ear. Matter is captured sound. What we call still and silent is still surrounded, indeed penetrated by sound which may be out of the audible frequencies of man's hearing. Without such sound, that which is form would disintegrate. By looking with understanding we will find the keys with which to unlock the silence and hence enable matter to sing again. Man, as an entire being, has this task and this responsibility.

(When considering the aspects of both man and woman in conjunction and as a unit, a Total one experience, the God within can begin to speak again. Then earthly sound can be a wonderful memory and have a creative meaning through the constant redemption that man; has at his command, redeeming sound as an answer to the question of the higher beings: "Do you understand what we wish to tell you so urgently?" "Yes, we are beginning to know and by listening will speak or , better still, sing in harmony with you.")

Out of such considerations will arise this new creation that will become real. The sounds of two human beings in total harmony will create forms which can be like a body inhabitable by a third being. Already we can photograph the forms sound creates when sounded and vibrated with certain media. (see Hans Jenny)?*

Now consider a poem spoken with real meaning, where the sounds are used to form the air around the speaker. With every sound he builds and sculpts a form – invisible to the physical eye. If he creates with awareness he is an architect of beauty. A room can be transformed into a temple, a place, a church. Mundane daily activities can thus be uplifted and sanctified by their surroundings.

Let us return to the string, on a straight line of light, held suspended between two poles. Without a body to resound in, this string cannot be heard. But now, if this string were suspended in a perfect sounding box, such as a sphere, we could see again that two (elements of form) are needed to create one (sound). The two elements could be called man and woman: thought and action, and *feeling* and action.

A thought is concise and can be expressed in logical terms; it is thereby also subject to crystallisation and on its own cannot live; it is dumb, as the lone string is dumb. A feeling can never be confined into a world of its own, even if it were possible to formulate it. The purpose of thought and feeling, or string and sound-body, is to *become*, in order to offer their entirety for the next stage – a third existence.

Is it thinkable that Father and Spirit, who also hold the Son, are actually the sphere and the line of light (string); that God is the eternal man/woman, one entity neither old nor young, never created and never subject to ending or beginning?

The heavenly spheres are the one constant, sounding creation, within this is held the well-mediated and real Word that has true pitch which man can never echo. The wonder is that both can, in total co-operation, create an even clearer sound and aspire to that WORD that creates WORLDS.

It is quite deliberate that the meaning of this text is not logical, precise and fully crystallised in words. By reading with open awareness, and seeking the meaning beyond the words, your own thoughts will blossom, your own doors will open and your world will expand.

Be content to listen in silence in those silent and dark temples.

Cymatics, Basilius Presse, Basle 1967, Hans Jenny.

Wait, don't rush . . . What . . . can you hear, answers which are not written down here? . . . Harken! This is still deeper, more profound . . . it contains the elements of awe, wonder and devotion. Be well aware of its non-perfection, incompleteness. Love is that which can still grow. Love is a still growing seed.

We have now found the two elements that are of the heavenly, creative, divine sounds of Apollo; we have only explored one side. What of the air that helps form sound? What of the breath that moves over the mouth of a reed? The reed limits the breath, the reed thus forming the breath into sound. Hence, all wind instruments are narrow pipes of varied length.

The power of such pipes is quite another aspect, it reacts on the physical and has known effects as well as unknown ones. Now we have sound captive in the pipe, flute, trumpet, etc., the wind blown in rebounding off the sides. And yet there is a special magic about it. Does it not also remind us strongly of the snake? The purely vertebral animal. The snake is the animal which has played an important part throughout the evolution of man, from the Garden of Eden into the Temple rites, in mythology and in many other connections bound up with the development of man. It has always represented consciousness growth. In man the spine is reminiscent of the snake and as we stand so much in the vertical position it causes consciousness to develop. Has not the pipe and the snake a very close link with music? The charm runs down the spine at times with a shiver of music.

Snake charmers have realised the effect of sound on the animal that resembles so closely our spine. The effect of the playing is unique. The snake is forced out of its horizontal position and raised quivering to its maximum vertical, to the tunes played, charming its own body into the only position it cannot hold without support by created sound.

The philosophy that stands behind this leads us to the ancient experience of the snake in the Garden of Eden, or the Kundalini. Subconsciously the charmer wishes to see how he can control that energy. That the raising of it is a dangerous game to play is well described in mythology and ancient books of temple wisdom. The art is to know what sound will inspire the snake to make a certain movement, and to learn the control of the experience of Kundalini.

It seems that the parts are now reversed. The string has become

Sound, Words, and Music in support of Colour Therapy

Human spine
Vertical

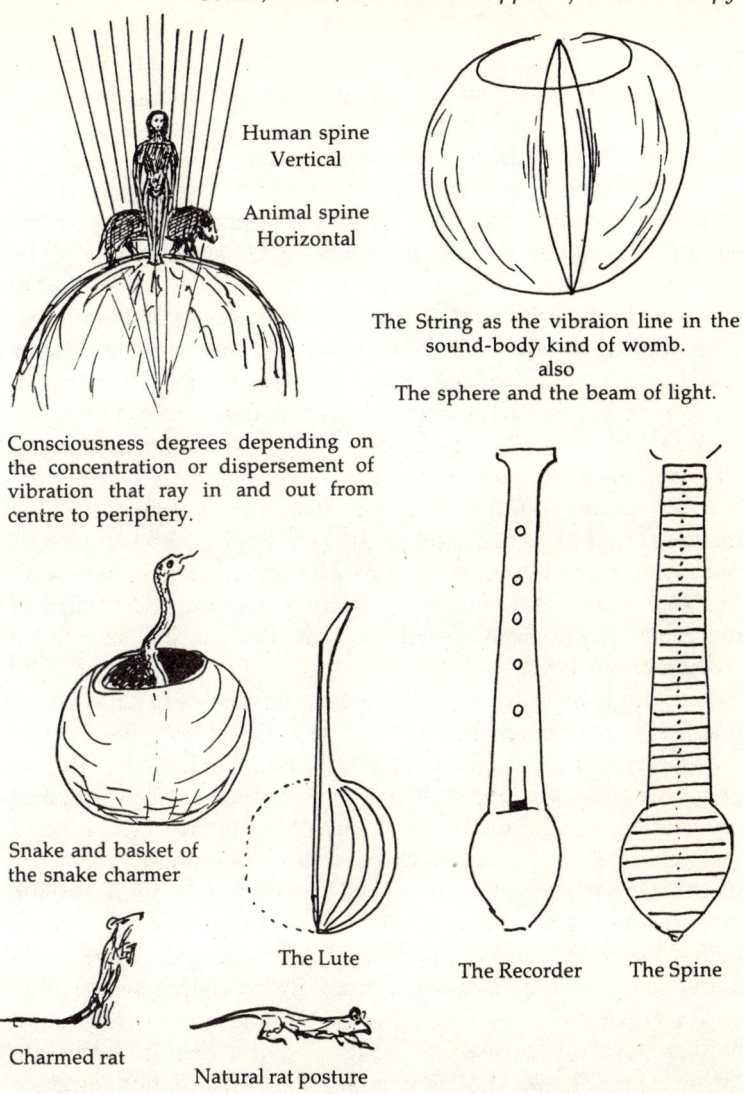

Animal spine
Horizontal

The String as the vibraion line in the sound-body kind of womb.
also
The sphere and the beam of light.

Consciousness degrees depending on the concentration or dispersement of vibration that ray in and out from centre to periphery.

Snake and basket of the snake charmer

The Lute

The Recorder

The Spine

Charmed rat

Natural rat posture

Fig. 2.6

the snake, the basket the sphere in which the sound could become audible. Thus, snake is now the woman aspect and basket the man. It is logical that a container needs to be found to hold such a very responsive and emotional creature as the snake.

41

Form, Sound, Colour and Healing

The pipes of organs can be so low in tone that only the vibrations are felt; certain low notes must be kept silent as their vibrations could demolish walls and destroy buildings. The power of sound thus captive in pipes can also kill.

On the other hand, the warm breath of man in pipes can generate charming sounds. The truest sounds are only forthcoming when the warmth and control of breath combine. Thus the sleeping snake is not raised into a dragon to kill man, but to be tamed and taught by man to become his servant. It is said that when George subordinated the dragon, the music of the spheres was heard by the Princess Elya who was in deep meditation during the battle. Seen from the higher planes, there is no sense in the killing of anything – there should be only the teaching of adversaries to co-operate in the real task.

After all, the serpent–dragon–snake is guardian of the treasures that lie beneath its sleeping body; he who truly tames this beast, using the power of music for unselfish gain, will soon find that the jewels reveal to him further teaching and healing of the errors made by non-co-operation. But the jewels will be spoken about later.

The simple recorder with the seven holes seems to have a close link with the human spine;* it also reflects the seven major chakras in the human body. It could be said that here the streams of sound energy pause in order to balance the ascending and descending vibrations. In a horizontal raying out at the level of these chakras we can experience what lives in human feeling and its contact with the environment; that which shines out into the physical world on these levels is a reflection of each human being. When they are in harmony the sounds make up the true being of man, the messenger from the invisible world who appears on the visible earth. Also, we become as men, incarnated beings who now speak in audible sound; before we were incarnate beings we spoke but could not be heard, nor could we be seen. Then through the voice of man will ring the sounds of the Word in truth.†

We know so well the beauty and reality of this, but we must also allow each to have much time for their tuning. The little

---

*See also Fig 2.6.
† According to the teachings of Rudolf Steiner 1861–1925.

Sound, Words, and Music in support of Colour Therapy

piece we may in the end be allowed to play needs a lifetime of tuning. The first long and arduous task is to learn to listen, and from this will come the sound that is the "pitch" to which we must tune our instrument. This tuning will not be just pitch, but also the very quality of sound, with immense dynamic properties.

But we may cheer up, because we know that all the teaching will be given, and will ensure our growing up to be in tune with the sounds of God. I do, however, feel that here in the sounds, is the ancient name of ABBA.* The sound of that name is the wisdom of God in the eternal essence of the one being for each other's sake, and this is its total purpose:

Almost universally man, in a spell of wonder and amazement, will say "Ah" (as in star), so that sound at the beginning is that great and original wonder, the awe, the amazement. It is then received and contained in the first "B" (the bowl, the vessel that offers to this sound a home). It knows that it is heard and loved. The confirmation is the second "B" which only exists because it will offer itself to the next process, being a kind of "basin" out of which the content can flow back into a renewed, but also enriched awareness, that it has said "A", Amen, Ave, A-B-B-A!

Man, in using sound, has learnt the art of pipe playing from Pan, the great Being who suffered to take hold of the earth so that man may be less bound by it. Pan knows that his greater self, on a higher level, is also Dionysis, and he, on another level, is the Christ. Man is now on the way to raising the snake, which, purposefully and not by chance is the animal of this earth that hands on a teaching to man; the teaching is often obscure and frequently a sacrifice. In the true intercourse between man and beast there is always the gain of more consciousness, although often subconsciously acquired. Therefore the story of the Pied Piper of Hamlin is a suitable ending to this chapter.

He, the piper, plays tunes that compel the rats to follow him. The dance is again so powerfully played that the animals dance on their hind legs all the way. Thus they have an experience of the narrow energy rays that are otherwise distributed over their horizontal spine. The trance they are compelled into is such that the final drowning is a self-preparation, a sacrifice to their own species. This is the prerogative of man; his clear consciousness is left when all the denser energies are distributed among stone,

Fig. 2.7

plant and animal, then man is free to stand. But he now also is responsible to the lower kingdoms and must remain mindful of their gifts. When each lower Kingdom shall be raised into the next higher experience of being raised into the vertical position. This then becomes a new possibility for a future aspect of evolution through Kundalini on that level. To the animal the upright posture is a Kundalini experience.

Kundalini to man is already on a much higher level and can often be so indescribably elevating an experience, that only he/she can know about it but not put it into words. The animal kingdom will go through stages which man has already conquered.

The total experience of sound on man, his being, his development, his state of consciousness, rising to the awareness of his divinity, is aimed to be a co-operation with ABBA; it is impossible to describe, even if time and space were there to write it down, all that can truly be felt about this task. We can only say that we know it is more than we can comprehend or see at present, but glimpses of it are pouring in ever faster.

Thus, the continuous flow of recognition, life and the dance that is life, is like the low tones of the organ pipe, fading out of our conscious experience and away into the realms beyond our capacity of hearing or as we now realise, of grasping as a totality as yet. What seems important is that by listening we should develop the right kind of sensitivity to make us better partners to the spiritual beings wishing to dance with us, but we are so often, still, so clumsy and so deaf.

Sound, Words, and Music in support of Colour Therapy

Therefore – Listen ... listen ... listen ...

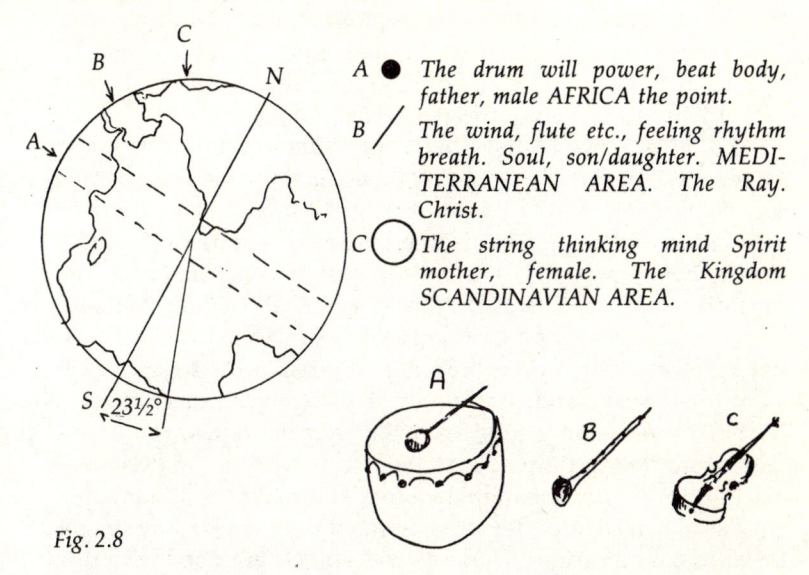

A ● The drum will power, beat body, father, male AFRICA the point.

B / The wind, flute etc., feeling rhythm breath. Soul, son/daughter. MEDITERRANEAN AREA. The Ray. Christ.

C ○ The string thinking mind Spirit mother, female. The Kingdom SCANDINAVIAN AREA.

Fig. 2.8

When we listen to music it seems that the thinking in man corresponds with the northern parts of this globe mainly the Scandinavian countries. The string music the melody instruments in this group have an affinity with these people.

In the moderate climate, the Mediterranean countries seem much more connected to the woodwind instruments they connect with the feeling and the emotional side of man.

For the equatorial countries, the drums and the rhythmic beat has an affinity with the will, the dance the stamping out of patterns and the throwing of spears. We can deduct from this that in a way such music can be applied to strengthen weaknesses in all people who need a music therapy to compliment the colour therapy approach. In the north the yellow colour if the intellect would be at home in the south European countries the orange and in the African countries the deep red.

Through the ages we have experienced old rhythms of working songs. The songs grew from the crafts in a particular countryside; fishermen or weavers, cobblers or tanners each had their own rhythms and songs which reflected the body movements necessary to each craft. They were well-known and children would grow up with these songs. Through the songs all feelings of estrangement were removed; fear complexes and hence violence or insanity, were not so common. It fact, violence is a kind of insanity that grows out of the inmusicality and discordant atmosphere of noise, instead of music.

Two cultural events have been changing this traditional folk singing. Firstly the advent of noisy machinery in factories, which has taken not only the craft out of the hands of men but also drowned their songs. This is one of the sad happenings which have robbed the people of this earth of their music making. The music making which was rhythmically linked to their craft and made artists, poets and craftsmen of them. So many have now not only lost their craft but also lost their art – the songs which were life creative and beautified their activity through music.

The second change has been the records, tapes, radio and television; "perfect music" can be had by getting the necessary equipment. So perfect and flawless that it makes us ashamed to try out our own imperfections. So men do not sing any longer because the homes and factories and schools are filled with this Hi-Fi Stereo, Quad, super sound. Few actualy realise that this so-called perfect sound is lacking one most vital part – and that is – the true harmonics (overtones). No recorded music at this time can claim to record the undistorted overtones; all recordings are suffering the total distortion of harmonics. Technically this appears because all the recording equipment is geared to 25,000 cycles per second. This goes just 3 to 10,000 cycles above the hearing capacity of human beings. For young babies and children it can be 22,000 c. per sec; for adult women, 18,000 c. per sec; for adult men 15,000 c. per sec.

We know how to translate the recorded sounds into meaningful music because we are able to link its likeness to our memory of live sound. Very young children and very sick people cannot do this. To them recorded sound is just a traumatic noise. It takes energy to translate, and experience of live sound, to make sense of recorded music.

How do we, however, get out of this dilemma? And do we have to condemn all recorded music?

There are recordings which have not had the top treatment. In other words, such recordings are unadulterated recordings of the actual moment when this orchestra, voice, instrument, was playing. No one went afterwards to put in echo, overriding depth of tone or brilliance of treble.

Such unadulterated tapes or records are sometimes really alive and carry a memory which is good and useful. In spite of this, for healing the ideal is live music, rather than recorded sounds. We cannot, today, eliminate all tapes, records, etc., but should try to be conscious of what we use and how we use music.

To work to music, to learn a language or a passage from history, with the aide of back-ground sound, seems to be a removing of the intellectual block. In cases where music is provided as a background to absorbing a subject matter, there comes with it a strange, often much delayed, side effect. This side effect can become very unpleasant and even disturbing. Months or years afterwards, music can turn up and go around our heads in such an uncontrolled fashion, that it can literally drive one insane.

What actually happens is that in such music-supported language learning, we are invited to become schizophrenic and split our mental intake into various levels of attention to sound and meaning. Consciousness is a very important part of human activity and needs direction by man's total, whole attention to a meaningful activity.

Sound, music, is the most wonderful experience; in using this we must become aware that it has vital orientation capacity when we use it well. All we need to do is to provide a foundation of love, enthusiasm, beauty and full attention to a moment of sound. All human beings are able to sound, sing and harmonize. Some may take a little longer than others – and so we must have a real patience.

That form, that divine image of God which the human being actually obeys is a very specific pitch. This pitch is so important to both mental and physical health, that the altering of it will not provide a healing capacity – even if the music is played exquisitely. I have met people who are given by birth a perfect sense of pitch and nowadays they suffer the agony of hearing most, almost all music played at too high a pitch. They must mentally transpose most of what they hear, this also amounts to an energy drain on them. The difference is just 8 c. per sec; but even this upsets the peaceful music effect and creates a subtle agitation instead of harmonious peace.

Music can aid memory in so far as through sound and relaxation, harmony can be brought; even right down into the molecular structure of all living beings. Plants, animals and humans react to music and I have a shrewd suspicion that also minerals vibrate and absorb sound.

So we go "back" if you like, to the old Pythagorean pitch, where the C below middle C is vibrating at 128 c. per sec (middle C at 256 c. per sec). Using this pitch, many so-called unmusical children and people can orientate their voices much better than under the normal concert pitch now in general use.

Memory enhancing comes about through the careful harmonizing of all environmental influences, including music, and at its most ideal point could be said to be Love. Create a place and an image that is full of love, to which a being can lend its wholeness, trust and know such beauty and such fullness of purpose, that nothing is left out – created, as it were, such a moment raises the attention of the human being into full co-operation; joy and love are being used to focus on that space in time. Then let this sink into the depth of forgetting and focus on another area.

Music-making with our voices is the most neglected and yet most creative activity, which can enhance our will to know, our will to be, our will to learn.

Take a group, a class, a company, of human beings and use the middle C at 256 c. per sec. Make them all hum in unison and teach them to listen to each other; listen, listen to their harmony being in harmony with the group. Then, introduce the note which is an octave above or below, and gradually bring about a harmony based on the C major key. Then, having got this harmony ringing, (paying no attention outwardly to anyone who may not as yet have quite got himself into harmony) you can start placing challenges into this by introducing the dominant 7th. Most of us, if not made conscious of it in an intellectual way, have a natural feeling for modulation and will soon develop in a group, a most beautiful feeling of sound relationship.

Long periods of completely improvised music is possible, which goes through most wonderful modulations; so groups can gradually become good at it, that the power of memory and listening is enhanced quite beyond all expectations.

Through this music-making we can heal society of the loss of music, out of which social harmony can grow again. Have courage to do this and let the imperfections sort themselves out so gently. All are able to learn this chanting:

> Chant ourselves back into
> Health and Harmony

Do this with your class every morning, before any of the intellectual learning is started.

It is like a prayer, a worship, a loving, a caressing of souls.

You can use here also the visualization of the five platonic solids in the following way:

Sound:	Form:	Colour:
Ah (as in Star)	Pentagondodecahedron	Violet
E (as in lay)	Octahedron	Yellow
I (as in Fee)	Tetrahedron	Red
O (as in low)	Icosahedron	Blue
U (as in you)	Hexahedron	Green*

An account of work and study at Hygeia Studios with advice for other "experiments".

With tape recorders, radio, TV and electronics, we are increasingly forgetting live music and, even more, the capacity of the human voice. In the course of three days a group of twenty-four people met to investigate the blending of human voices. They found that, prepared by an introduction which opened the world of sound to them, the idea of music became far more comprehensive than they had previously thought possible.

Theo Gimbel introduced the theme of Universe–Earth–Man as a unity, and indicated that man, the one who has to stand alone, does not harmonise and has no natural affinity with his environment. However, by his consciousness he can so attune himself by love that he can almost identify himself with his task of learning to hold the balance in all things. Man is a highly adaptable being and, in cases of real need and when deprived of the complete experience of the whole man he can, in fact, change "sex".

*Very valuable here are the visual aid: The Five Platonic Solids as a mobile available through Hygeia Publications, Brook House, Avening, Tetbury GL8 8NS.

Theo related an experience of his years as a prisoner-of-war in Russia. The prisoners had brought together a group of men who could remember music and, on cement-bag paper, they wrote melody and harmony. Indeed, the total score of operas was reconstructed and corrected from memory – Aïda, Cavalleria Rusticana and Die Fledermaus. When it was necessary, some of the prisoners sang soprano parts in falsetto voices. Within less than a year they had several "girls", whose speech became that of women, long hair grew, and beards needed less and less shaving. Emotionally and physically they grew more closely to resemble the so desperately lacking female element. That this also resulted in homosexuality was, of course, only too natural. In performances, concerts and operas, they enjoyed and totally supported these relationships and three was an air of beauty and reality about them. Even Theo, at one stage, felt it would take very little to change emotionally into a woman. He feels, on looking back, that he was very lucky to know such deep soul experiences.

Man is the ever adaptable and always non-specialised "animal" who can consciously choose either the agony or the ecstasy.

During the initial stages of investigation into the sound of human voices it was found that neither the use of chime bars, lyres, flutes, nor trying to follow and then interpolate on a theme hummed by a member's lead, allowed people to harmonise in both voice and spirit mind.

It was suggested that it would be worthwhile attempting to become attuned to each other by maintaining a silence, and "listening" to it, until someone felt so attuned that he/she could very slowly, and carefully begin to hum one or more notes. Other people could then join whoever happened to lead as and when they felt attuned.

This suggestion bore remarkable results. After a period of silence one voice began to hum a fairly low note and gradually and most carefully, others joined in. During a period of approximately ten minutes the sound varied from a quiet hum to a crescendo with the sound of "a" as in star), and included a marvellous blend of bass, soprano, alto, tenor and mezzo-soprano voices. Subsequent discussion led to a repetition of this "practise". After a number of repeats it became evident that not only were the initial silences becoming longer, but also subse-

Sound, Words, and Music in support of Colour Therapy

quent silences were occurring. It was also noticed that certain rhythms were appearing in the form of crescendo and decrescendo and that the "pieces" were longer lasting.

The foregoing situation was not arrived at by constant repetition. The "practises" were dispersed, between lectures on Sound, over a period of two days.

After a "practise" which occurred at the end of the first session on the third day, one person tentatively mentioned that he had become so attuned to the environment and the voices, that he had, for the last few "practises" seen certain forms and colours in his mind's eye. This comment broke through any remaining barriers to complete attunement; well over half the members stated they had seen forms and colours but had not felt sufficiently attuned to express themselves.

At the end of further "practises" members suggested that verbal descriptions of what they had "seen" was perhaps not the best method of expression. The idea was put forward that drawing would be a better medium. For the remainder of the day after each "practise" members went to the blackboard without being asked, and either sketched or wrote what they had "seen" or felt. The following illustrations are some of the many produced by members. See colour pages (v–viii).

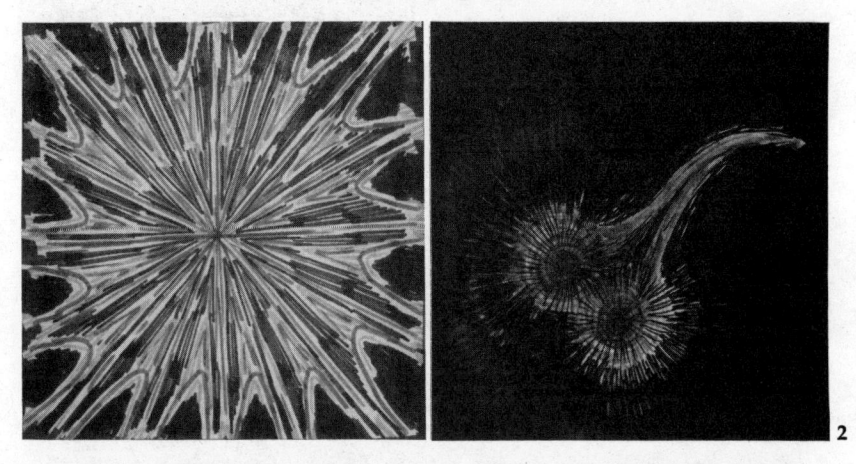

1. From an indigo blue background, a golden star spreading until it filled the whole field of vision, and with rays which shone more and more brightly. Finally, from the star centre there appeared an almost white star, partly radiating, which eventually took on a very fine magenta, peach-blossom,

Form, Sound, Colour and Healing

hue. The whole appeared to be brilliantly expanding and breathing, and even after the "practise" ceased, remained in the mind's eye of the person.
(the Star)

2. From two violet centres, brilliantly radiating, and at the edges flecked with colours, predominantly gold, white and turquoise, two adjoining half wings extended to form a tail. Initially this appeared in the far distance, and then travelled towards the person in a way which was likened to the progress of a comet. Unlike a comet, this did not break up into the void but remained in the minds eye of the person. (Comet)

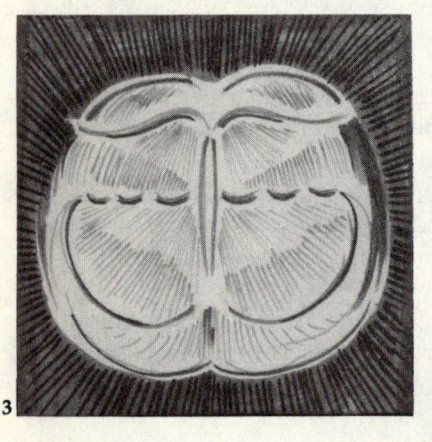

3. Columns rising to vaulted roofs, the whole having a church/temple appearance. Gradually the vault came into view and was seen to be open to the sky. Initially the vault had a base and two sloping sides, but finally a faint image of a dove appeared in the sky to close the opening and form a pentagonal shape. (Place of worship)

4. A dewdrop shape, mainly coloured red and orange, appeared to be hovering in a vessel. The whole vessel edged with gold was illuminated in etheric colours, and was felt to be containing the energy of the sound created by the "practise". (Dewdrop)

5. Forms of ever-changing shape appeared out of a deep midnight blue. The forms pulsed with energy and were fresh green and white in colour. Changes in the rhythm of the "practise" were responsible for the variations in the shapes of forms. One person likened the drawing to a pulsating rosette.
(Rhythm-Rosette)

6. A member wrote the word PEACE on the blackboard. Alongside the word another member sketched a dove hovering in the sky. The member who had written PEACE said she had only "seen" the word, but the dove's outspread wings and radiating lines beautifully fitted her conception of peace.

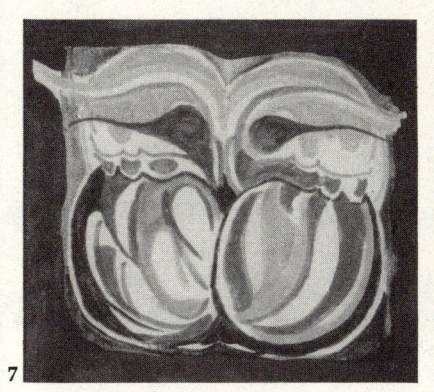

Sound, Words, and Music in support of Colour Therapy

7. Towards the end of the practises it was noticed that within the majority of sketches the shape of wings could be discerned. Generally the wings were to be seen in parts of sketches having the more etheric magenta, peach-blossom colours. Theo, who is a talented artist, without explanation drew wing shapes in the positions where one would draw the brow, eyebrows, mouth and chin of a human face. Before he had completed the mouth the sketch was immediately recognizable to all members as being one of a human face. When, by adding an outline and colouring, he finished the sketch, most members agreed that they had perceived the final image of what was being drawn long before the final touches were given to the sketch. All could see that this was a human face of angelic character; a smiling but watchfully concerned face. During subsequent discussion it was discovered that in a number of the sketches containing wings, the vague images of similar faces were discernable.

During a discussion in the penultimate session Theo told of his experience of the Harmony of the Spheres, and related them to the previous session. In 1947, as a prisoner of war in Russia, he twice experienced the harmony of the spheres:

"I was meditating on the past events which led to my captivity in 1945. I lay on the bare planks of my place in the hut on 4th January and 14th February of that winter. It was bitterly cold, some 35°–40°C below zero. The chatter of my hut mates (about 50) was fading away as my concentration went to the many events ever further away from the present moment . . . then began this sounding of unaccountable tones, blending in ever more beautiful harmonies, and leading over discords to new keys. But all happened at the same time.

There was no harmony, nor was there discord, but there was both. The Spheres were singing in quite unearthly sounds. Not the voice of a human being, but of an angel, was speaking through this heavenly experience: "Thou are permitted to see the most beautiful body which is cast into the ether world". Then it faded out as my fiancée called me back. (She was at that time 3000 miles west of my position.)

From the three days of investigation the following conclusions were reached:

A group, by carefully listening to each other, can obtain a common image. This image is not apparent during the first few meetings but, once attunement is reached, develops rapidly throughout the group.

Crescendo parts of the practises always gave the feeling of group harmony, but it is during these periods that the greatest difficulty in "listening" is experienced.

Instruments hinder attunement between people who have no musical attainments. This is not the case with a group of professional musicians. During one discussion the Raphael painting of Saint Cecilia was mentioned. Raphael depicts the saint of music turning away from the sounds made by earthly instruments, and her companions looking, as if deaf, at the broken pipes and lutes lying uselessly on the ground. Saint Cecilia is listening to the Harmony of the Spheres. Later, in her martyrdom, she was transported into the arts of the God-Goddess of the sound-creating fields.

Sound, Words, and Music in support of Colour Therapy

We can listen to the Harmony of the Spheres and realise that the seldom-used psychic capacities of man can be fruitfully developed, and the personal attunement to each other here on earth can be seen and experienced as a peace, spreading and balancing the harmony of the Christ by manifesting in this experience our daily life and thereby following our Master of all Masters.

This aspect of sound will be further developed at Hygeia as part of the courses and research, and it is also felt to be much of what Father Andrew Glazewski* was striving towards – the listening and the experience of music for all who can listen.

A–Z of names and words

1 Introduction into the area

Sound, 'music', has not only a pleasing, or sometimes also disrupting influence upon our ears, but has energies that are beginning to be found working in our subconscious being. Sound can, in other words, help us to feel well or ill.

Since sound can also move by its vibrations fine matter, such as sand, iron fillings, powder, or water, in short anything which is able to move or able to be moved, we must consider its very important implications from many different aspects. It finally emerges that there is nothing which cannot ultimately be moved by sound.

Recent experiments and findings through research have shown that sound is capable of composing new structures or breaking down existing ones.*

---

* *The Music of Crystals, Plants and Human Beings*, Father A. Glasewski, Radio Perception September 1951. Now available through Hygeia Publications, Avening, Tetbury GL8 8NS.

* *Cymatics*, Hans Jenny, Volumes I and II, Basilius Presse, Basle, 1971.

2   Sound and Form

This study shows that sound is indeed a medium which should be studied to understand how it can influence our health patterns and personality. In the work of Hans Jenny we can see how the pitch controls the patterns and that according to low pitch wider and larger patterns appear, and the higher tone ranges make very fine and intricate patterns. Thus, from low pitch, which is inaudible to the human ear, to infinite high pitches, also beyond the human hearing, sound can control form which determines to some extent our health. Considering the pure sound or the sound coloured by the form or method of how it is made audible, the human voice can imitate almost all sounds of animals or instruments. All instruments are really one of the infinite possible sounds extracted out of the total sound field. It is said that the human voice has more overtones and (inaudible) harmonics than any other sound. According to the specific colour and timbre of any sound, the finer forms and structures change even if only so small that we do not see the difference. In some way the very fine changes in quality and colours act upon the subconscious area, whereas the very low tones have power to change structure very rapidly and drastically.

From fatigue to severe illness and even death, sound can have tremendous influences upon the life pattern and mental, emotional and physical well being of minerals, plants, animals and humans. When we mention the changes in minerals we can say that vibrations (sound) bring about what is known as metal-fatigue. Due to molecular structure changes matter can lose its inner patterns, so that it finally can fall into dust, break or change into a new structure.

3   Intervals, Rhythms, Repetition

With the rhythmic change of a sound and the change of pitch between two sounds we find a clear alteration of alertness according to the interval. Some intervals are pleasing and create a peaceful mood in people, others are rousing and some are even highly disturbing. Out of the intervals and the rhythmic element as well as the change of pitch is finally created a melody, a tune.

These can be happy, slow, soothing or disturbing. It is known that music which contains an overbalance of dischords will, by way of repetition over a period of time, undermine the human mental and emotional harmony. Most people have a very fine feeling for music which has a pleasing and healing influence, or the opposite.

4   Harmonics Distortion

Live sound, music made by song or any instrument heard by the listener directly reaches the ear with all the harmonics and overtones which are inaudible in fact, not distorted. As soon as we record sound, whether tape or radio or records, we lose more than is usually accepted by most of us. There lies an indication that tissue seems to lose response with age and that the male is slightly denser than the female.

Very young children and very sick adults should not be subjected to recorded music as they both lack the capacity to make real sense of the heard sound.

We adults, in the so called normal situation, have enough memory stored up of the live sound so that when we listen to recorded music we subconsciously correct all the distortions. This requires an energy which we have to supply. Hence children have not yet got it and sick people cannot raise the energy to do it. To both these areas of human beings the sound they hear is a traumatic noise.

5   History of Ancient Knowledge

In the ancient Sanskrit and Hebrew as well as the old Greek use of sound there has always been a knowledge that all sounds which are spoken by man through the words of his/her language have a 'power', power to create energy to make available certain resources which lie hidden in the specific sound of an 'A' such as in st*a*r or f*a*r. In the course of cultural changes the development of races and the path of evolution we go through the early, middle and late period. In the early stages we can experience the time to grow, the middle stages when activity is being the predominant factor and the late stages when the thoughts of intelligence fill the last period. It is in this moment when we should remember the original growth of feeling because in this period is embedded the seed of resurrection. In most cultures we have at that point lost the energy to internalise the work where we could find a new beginning. So we have lost the power of the word, which once, as St. John puts it, "was creative".

6   Todays New Aspects

We can now look at this area with new eyes, understand it also on a new level and build it into our modern concepts.

Into each age are born those teachers who can help us to develop the next step along the journey. Using now the ancient knowledge together with the teachings which were given at the beginning of this century by Rudolf Steiner we can begin to use the meaning of the sounds again and build up what may become a new way to rediscover our energy. In the names of people and the use of the given name there are the ways by which we can have first an understanding of our name, secondly make a new relationship with this our name, and thirdly find again the energies which we could not recognise earlier.

Through the work which Steiner introduced in 1913 called, "Eurythmy as Visible Speech", he handed to this age a new understanding of the ancient wisdom.

Thus, our names can become again filled with energy to which we can have access.

7   Personal Growth, Changes and Development

When we again understand the individual energy that flows through our letters that make up our name we will discover a beautiful mandala of sacred nourishment to our growth. We will be able to come to terms with that pattern and the intentions which originally stood in this name, as it were, secretly hidden and protected. It is then time, and usually the right time, to hear this meaning and to begin to use the name as a key to our lives. There are people today who have great difficulty coming to terms

Sound, Words, and Music in support of Colour Therapy

with their names. A name is a challenge and will often demand of the bearer to live up to its potentials. Some find this hard to let happen. Others may prefer not to be called Michael – but rather Mike, not Peter but Pete, not Thomas but Tom. In all these abbreviations we find the diminishing of the original capacity, that the name has in its full meaning. In a way it is a cutting short or a forestalling of the development which lies in the name.

8 Fine Vibratory Quality of each Alphabet Letter

*A = + Awe, wonder, reverence, openness.
            – Open to all things, thereby also open to indecision and/or confusion.
B = + Containing, protecting, holding.
            – Closing up, keeping secret, mean.
C = + Light, air (magic).
            – Dispersing, breaking up.
D = + The doing of the deed, dedication.
            – Finalising, suppressing.
E = + Linking between heaven and earth, truth, uprightness.
            – Pride, overbearing, egocentred.
F = + Enthusiasm, flow, firey.
            – Disrespect for others, unaccommodating.
G = + Creating space, freedom, grace.
            – Selfish, vanity, self-engrandisement.
H = + Quick, active, enthusiastic.
            – No time for others, mocking.
I = + Gentleness, kindness, considerate.
            – Indecision, weakness, sloppy.
J =   Mystery sound which can transmute energies.

---

* All sounds must be used in their phonetic pronunciation.
+ Positive,   – Negative implications.

Form, Sound, Colour and Healing

K = + Clear, clean, precise decision.
     − Cutting, abrupt, insensitive.
L = + Light, love, life, blossoming.
     − Overflowing, imposing.
M = + Transmuting, creative, movement, exchanging, seeing both sides of a situation.
     − Restlessness, impatience.
N = + Discernment, capacity to say 'no', ability to choose well.
     − Crushing ideas.
O = + Protection, keeping in love.
     − Greed, possessiveness
P = + Questioning, enquiring, fun, joy.
     − Puzzle, disjointedness.
Q = + On the spot, awareness.
     − Immobility, fixed in love.
R = + Will to act, energy, movement to do things.
     − Rushing in where angels fear to tread, inconsiderate, self-willed.
S = + Magic, achievement of difficult things.
     − Power, negative magic.
T = + Anchoring, making a foundation, determination, finalising.
     − Fixed, cool and calculated, piercing, hurting.
U = + The channel, conducting energy, mediator.
     − Dissolving energy, restlessness.
V = + Par cé val, going through the path, acceptance of destiny, confidence.
     − Pride, resistance to learn.
W = + Pliable, mobile, healing, flow with steadfastness.
     − Weak, easily lead, wavering, indecisive.
X = + Precision, surity, confidence.
     − Static, closed in, non-communicative.
Y =   Mystery sound.
Z = + Magic with absolute firmness.
     − Misuse of power and knowledge.

A =   (as pronounced in 'able' or 'stable')
   +   Concentration, bringing to a point
   −   Shutting in, fixed.

9   Phonetics

In each language we have the pronunciation problem which on the other hand offers mobility to the spoken word. The indications in the preceeding alphabet are always subject to the fine colouring of each sound as it changes a little by its preceeding or following sound. Also, the repetition of a letter will reconfirm the original energy with all the preceeding sounds to strengthen this, for example: 'Barbara'. We have a mandala which starts out as containing and protecting into the wonder and awe, then to will and actively do. The second time B-A-R appears to confirm this and concludes in awe and wonder.

10   Diminutives

All the diminutives are areas which have to be seen as two activities.
   (a) The loving expression, however, a wish to keep small and retain the original sweetness of the 'baby'.
   (b) The restriction to let the full potential grow and see equality in a partnership, neither subordinate nor domineering.

It is in its right place with the small child and should at the right moment be allowed to be changed to the full name. This can be a growing point and acceptance into the circle of equality, co-being instead of the one who cannot take his rightful place in self-determination.

11   Changes

Many people feel that they are unhappy or not really in tune with their given name. Some have more than one name so they have a choice perhaps. Others need to seek for a new name. In this case it is wise to be guided insofar as it is good to think of it yourself and get a quiet feeling for it. The getting used to another name should be carefully approached. You can link it with your original name where the now chosen one is placed quietly behind the given one. After a time you may or may not feel unhappy with it. If you like it you can swop around and make out of Mary-Elizabeth Elizabeth-Mary. In time, it is still good to drop Mary and be Elizabeth instead of Mary. It must be said that there will be an energy change according to what you have chosen. Sound will, as you remember, have an impact upon your being and can make good vibrations come to you or discordant ones. *You* must gauge this and sharpen your feelings for it.

12   Conclusions, Rhythms

Now you may with this whole approach try to get a new look into what the word means. Take names of places, or houses, or societies and see how the energy patterns work out in relation to the word you are using. Behind the common meaning will arise the hidden meaning of very vast fields, concepts which you were not aware of previously. Look at this with joy and a sense of discovery. Take it easy, make no dogmatic way of a fanatical kind out of it. When everything is said and done it is one of the thousand ways of life as a whole.

Vibration and Pitch

This vibration is almost half a tone below the present day concert pitch. Making middle C 256 c. per sec. or A above middle C 432 c. per sec. – Maria Rendolf Neusheller of Dornach has made a deep study of the indications given by Rudolf Steiner. She has found that the pitch can either pacify or agitate the human being.

In my research I find that young children who are taught music at school are frequently said to be unmusical because they cannot find their notes easily. Using however the old Pythagorean pitch, as referred to above, many of them can suddenly find their pitch much more easily. The whole body of each human being is

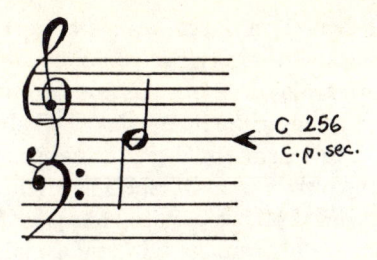

Sound, Words, and Music in support of Colour Therapy

C 256 c.p.sec.

aligned to the pitch of 256 c. per sec. for middle C. Children are most unspoilt and find that pitch natural. Therefore they will readily adjust to this and not get lost because of our modern 'manipulation' of pitch.

Intervals, Rising and Falling

Now as to the special use of intervals. The diatonic scale (based on C 128 c. per sec.) builds up in its rising structure to 1024 c. per sec. and taking into account the skull even to 2048 c. per sec. The total spine including sacrum and skull makes up 5 octaves, from 64 c. per sec. to 2048 c. per sec.

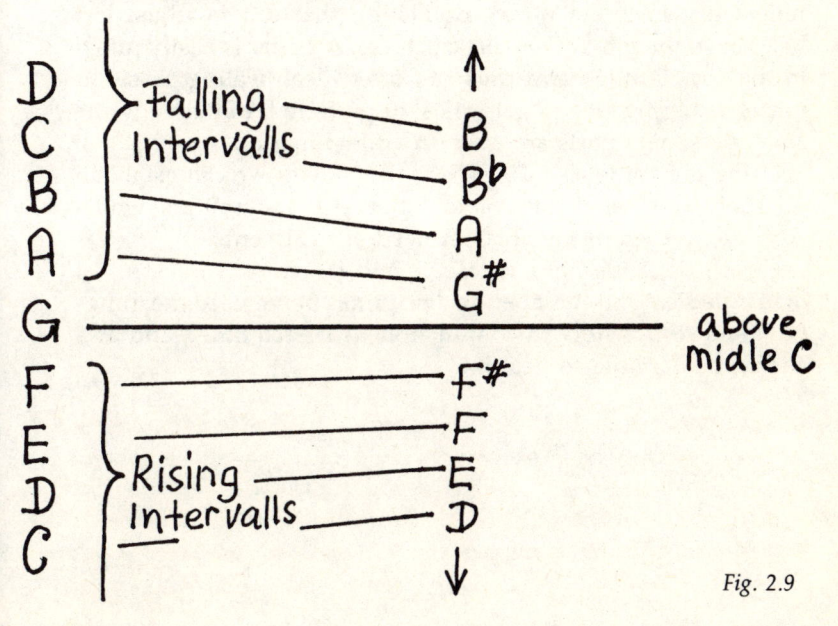

Fig. 2.9

The chromatic scale is a descending (falling) scale. Thus we have a wonderful way to experience balance and the swing out on the falling intervals from the centre of our spine (Dorsal vertibrae 5) making the prime interval of G–G above C 256 c. per sec. expanding up to a dem.5th C 1024 c. per sec. down to below this C. Branching out below Dorsal 5 we widen to inclining intervals ending with C (128 c. per sec.) to a pure 5th above this C (C–G). The intervals will of course widen if we take the Sacrum as 8 vertebrae condensed ending then with 64 c. per sec. on C, below middle C.

Composing Healing Sound

Using such intervals we may get compositions made which can be of a healing nature. This is then used in conjunction with Colour Therapy Treatment. The scales of colour and the scales of music are complementary energies and have a healing capacity.

The interval(s) of any vertebrae which is discovered to be out of balance is found by dowsing. These intervals can then be used in conjunction with harmonies and or accompanying tones repeatedly so to set off an oscillation that can re-adjust lost balance in the molecular cell structures. A guitar is easily tuned to the correct pitch and thus can offer ideal healing music. It needs some practice to get this skill perfected, but already the small personal efforts are a worthwhile pursuit.

Using the spine as a diagnostic instrument we can establish not only the beneficial colours, but also the sounds which coincide to each of the areas in need of treatment.

Health depends on a wholistic and co-operative system of many medical and therapeutic disciplines being used meaningfully and responsibly in conjunction with each other, and as a supplementary aid to health.

Form, Sound, Colour and Healing

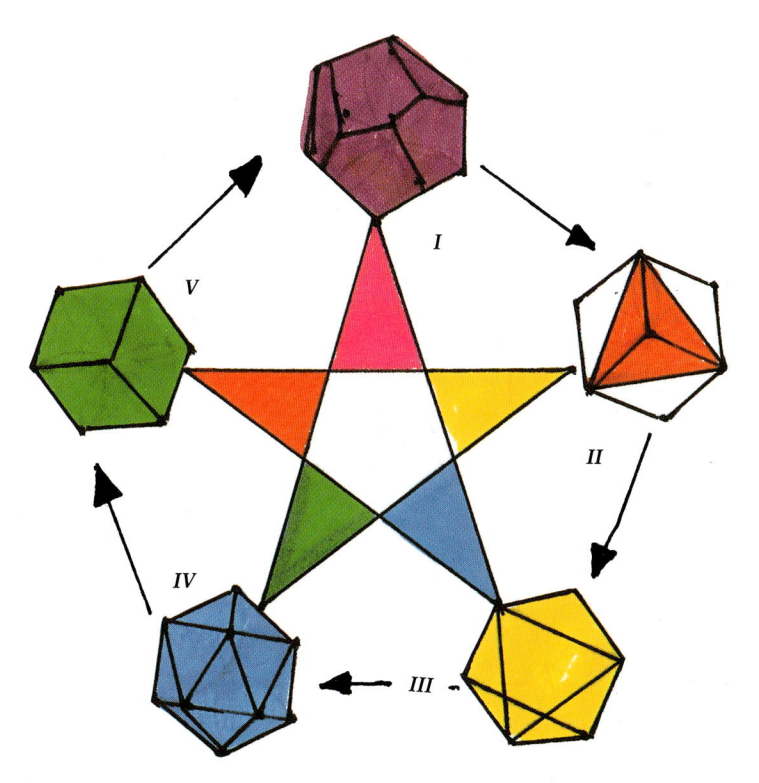

Fig 1.4 see page 13

(i)

Form, Sound, Colour and Healing

ABOVE *Fig 1.13 see page 17*
BELOW *Fig 1.15 see page 18*

Form, Sound, Colour and Healing

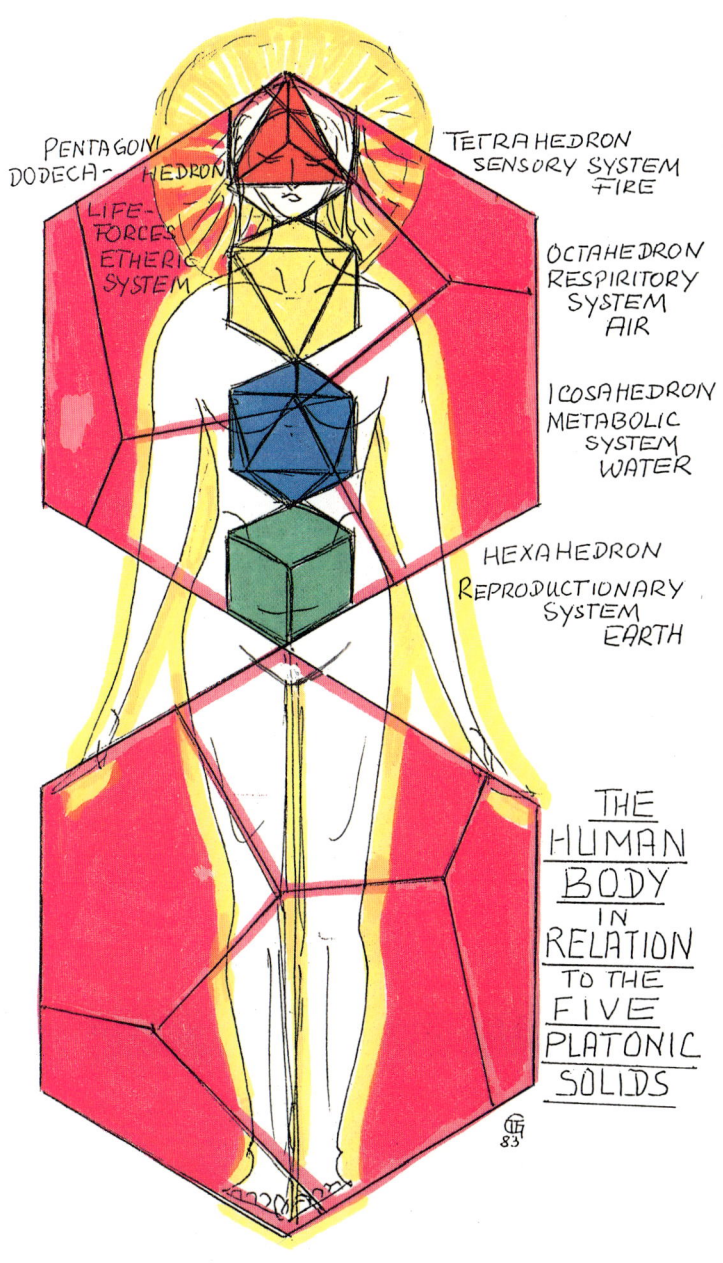

PENTAGONI DODECA-HEDRON
LIFE-FORCES ETHERIC SYSTEM

TETRAHEDRON
SENSORY SYSTEM
FIRE

OCTAHEDRON
RESPIRATORY SYSTEM
AIR

ICOSAHEDRON
METABOLIC SYSTEM
WATER

HEXAHEDRON
REPRODUCTIONARY SYSTEM
EARTH

THE HUMAN BODY IN RELATION TO THE FIVE PLATONIC SOLIDS

Fig 1.16 see page 19

(iii)

Form, Sound, Colour and Healing

Fig 1.20 see page 22

Fig 1.21 see page 25

Form, Sound, Colour and Healing

1 *see page 51*

2 *see page 51*

Form, Sound, Colour and Healing

3 *see page 52*

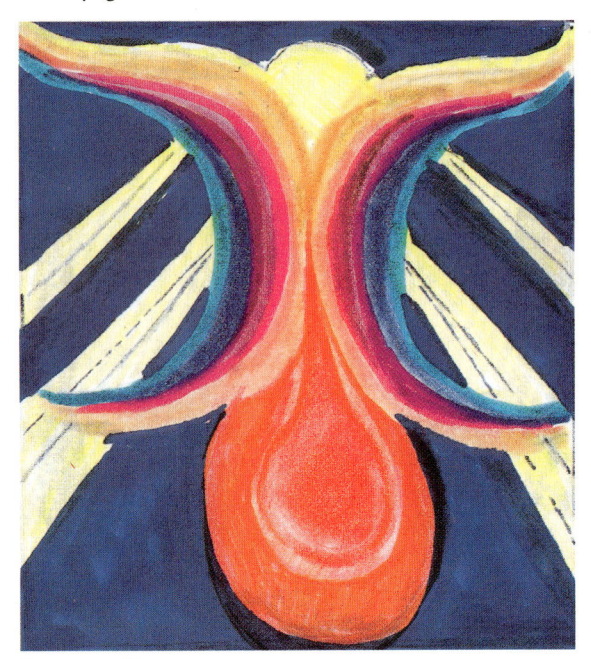

4 *see page 52*

Form, Sound, Colour and Healing

5 *see page 53*

6 *see page 53*

Form, Sound, Colour and Healing

7 *see page 53*

8 *see page 53*

(viii)

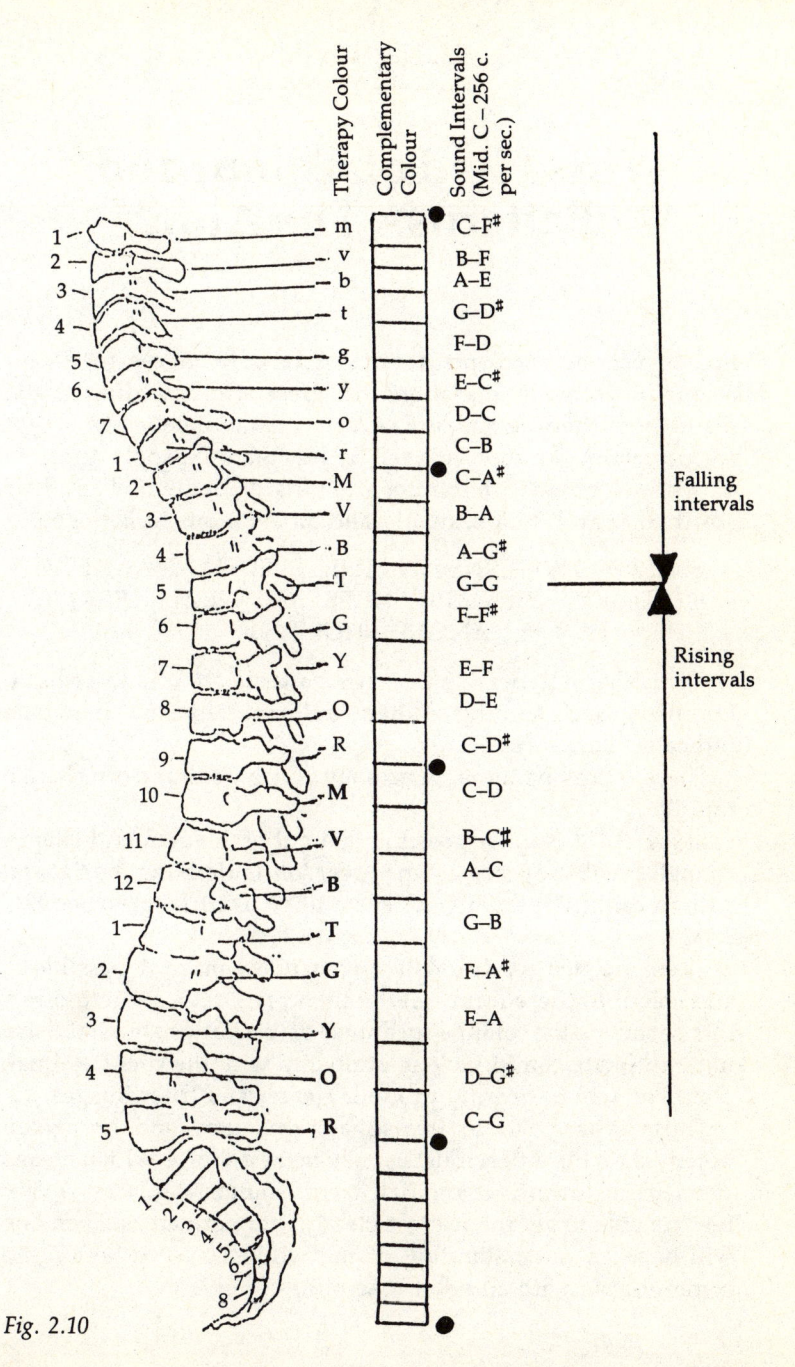

Sound, Words, and Music in support of Colour Therapy

Fig. 2.10

65

Chapter 3

This Field of Colour and Patterns – The Aura

People respond to colours not in general only but can cope with colour in decor, illumination and dress also according to the maturity of their personality. A very mature person can accept colours which are soon rejected by less mature people. It has to do with self esteem, their inner thoughts about themselves, their spirituality and their sexuality and all emotions in between.

ENERGY PATTERNS IN THE ELECTRO-MAGNETIC FIELD OF BIOSUBSTANCES (MINERAL, PLANT, ANIMAL, HUMAN)

Normally, in general, all energy patterns are a kind of light, luminous and shining. When dullness appears then this indicates blockages.

These energy patterns are actually very mobile and can change rapidly.

In Fig. 3.1 it is quite possible that out of the diamond shapes triangles will appear, as the over or underlying horizontal pattern can make the images seem to be like triangles. See Fig. 3.11.

There are two conditions which actually make it possible to add colour to these forms (a) the therapists dedication to direct this 'vision' to the colour appearance or (b) the need to establish a more intimate comfortable relationship with the client, animal, plant etc. will frequently produce clearer and truer images.

Those who wish to investigate this area and are given potentials at the outset must usually make a choice, which means specialising towards colour or towards sound awareness. A very few are able to get themselves clearly into both areas. Each one will have an understanding of the whole so as to be able to communicate with all other disciplines.

This Field of Colour and Patterns – The Aura

What is actually now acknowledged by so many scientists is that we must work towards a wholistic concept which allows the many specialised fields to come into conversation. This means that we have to train people not only as extremely good technologists, biologists, metallurgists etc. but as qualified specialists who also have enough understanding of the area surrounding their particular science to grasp the wholistic concepts. To raise the present standard of communication between the various disciplines we must accept the need for a wholistic approach.

In the final analysis we should remind ourselves to ask the question: "For whom do we want to make progress – for whom do we research into more advanced styles of life?" The answers may be many, as many as there are thinking people on this planet, but my own guess is the majority of answers will read: "For the sake of people who will live with the results of our findings today and onwards".

Into this field, which is about the size of the completely outstretched arms and in a three dimensional way all around the body, are inscribed all the patterns of the Aura laid out in the sketches. There must be uncounted others but of these we are not yet aware. Each pattern holds within it the total pattern of the whole if we could see it that closely.

Fig. 3.1

Energy lines frequently cross over, creating a diamond shape-like pattern, especially where there are ductless glands, geodes, flower buds, seeds. These diamond shape patterns can be very open or very dense. See Fig. 3.7. Buds show a delicate, usually very transparent energy tendency to be of a bluish colour, turquoise. Seeds show a stronger, less translucent energy, tending to be a reddish in colour.

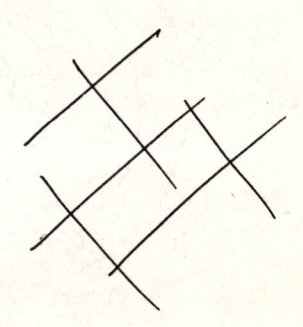

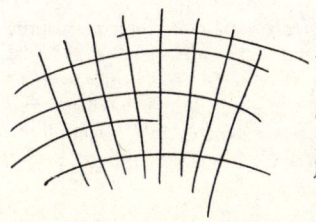

Fig. 3.2

Usually over-laid, but may also be under laying and is also the above kind of structure. This grid of energy usually surrounds and/or focuses on a centre. See Fig. 3.5.

Form, Sound, Colour and Healing

Fig. 3.3

This is usually in motion; if very gently moving all seems to be well; but if over activated it can spin to the dangerous point of disturbing the equilibrium of the entity which is its anchor point.

Fig. 3.4

Energy as in Fig. 3.4 is circulating in a spiral shape around areas which hold potentially very important places where a physically unexpressed power point is located, or where previously there were energies that are now asleep, or where future development can take place.

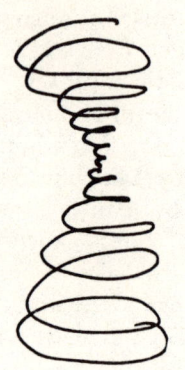

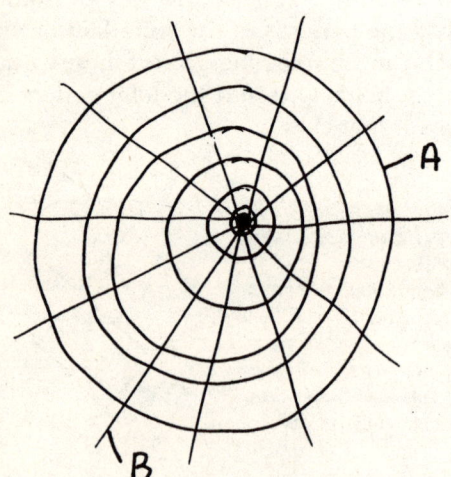

Fig. 3.5

All visible objects have two major radiations one which we will call for the sake of definition horizontal (A) the other vertical (B). A is the energy which protects and provides an outer skin (shield) around the physical centre like seeds or an egg.

This Field of Colour and Patterns – The Aura

Fig. 3.6

Some of the extra-terrestrial energies can manifest themselves in forms like rays of light, usually Gold on a Violet-Blue background with almost up to White fine lines inscribed. Although this is not an Aura field which shows itself in physically incarnate energy patterns it can appear to those especially gifted to perceive.

We should not need to be jealous as all thinking people have the capacity to know potentially all. The only question is what have you yourself dedicated to know and understand, and what you want to strengthen. All must specialise so as to become clear and useful in their fields. What matters is that we know enough of all the areas which are adjacent to ours to be able to communicate.

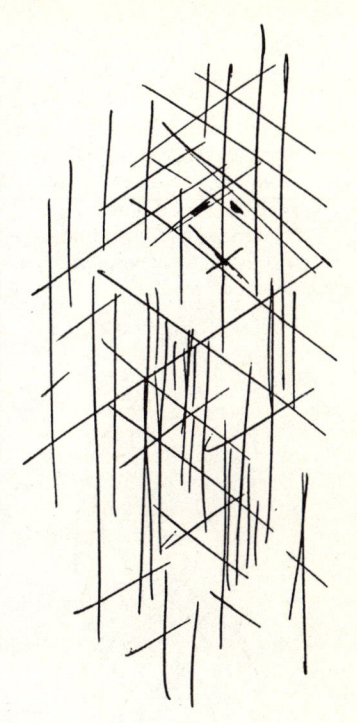

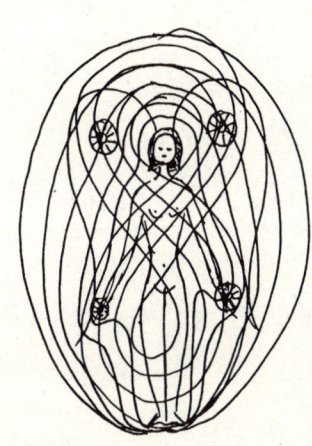

Fig. 3.7

This is a sketch showing as man of the 'normal' energy forms around a human structure as can be drawn without producing an unintelligible maze of patterns. Around the physical body is placed the etheric sheath, see 3.8, then the horizontal pattern, see Fig. 3.2, then the vertical ones; the spirals (8) mainly at shoulders, hips wrists and ankles then the four 'eyes' within the upper part of the Aura, the centres of the etheric 'wings', see Fig. A. Within this is also the lemniscate pattern, see Fig. B.

All this builds up to a most wonderfully rich energy pattern that can show the potentials of a being. For obvious reasons not all is always perceived at the same time as it becomes, as they say 'too much' to be able to comprehend as a person now in a physical body.

Form, Sound, Colour and Healing

Fig. 3A

Only a little by little will open, so that we may be safe. Take the trouble and use a completely calm mind and visualise all this as perfectly possible. And then use humility, gratitude and love as on offering to the invisible world that has give us the insight. When we study the structures in physics we will see many forms which are reminiscent of Aura patterns.*

Fig. A

Fig. 3B/Fig. 3C

In conclusion of Fig. 3.7 it frequently occurs that the triangular forms appear which bring together the horizontal, the vertical and the lemniscate patterns thus we arrive at an image something like Fig. C.

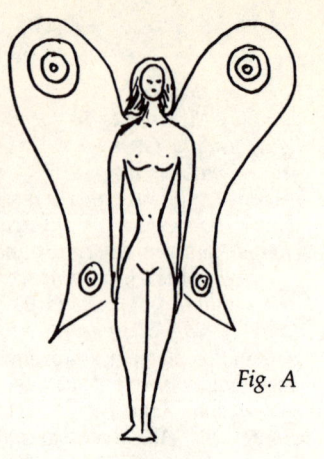

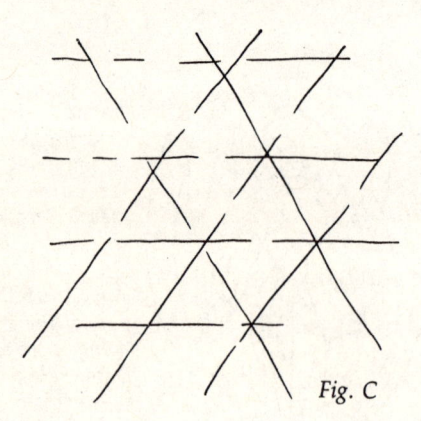

Fig. B

Fig. C

[*1] 'The Aura' by Walter J. Kilner, BA, MBCantab, MRCP etc. Late electrician at St Thomas' Hospital, London.
'Explorations of Consciousness' and 'The Loom of Creation'. Edited by Dennis Milner. Authors: James Binns PhD, Harry Dean MSc, Brian Meredith PhD, Dennis Milner DSc, Edward Smart.

This Field of Colour and Patterns – The Aura

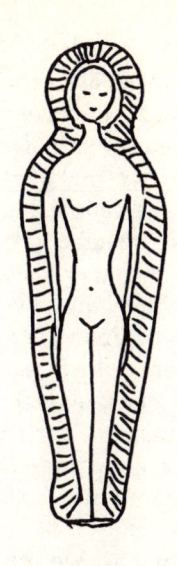

Fig. 3.8

The immediate energy field around a bio-structure is slightly denser and known as the etheric sheath. This sheath moulds itself very closely to the physical form. In minerals and plants it is fairly static and does not change in density. However, plants show a change during 24 hours from being larger at night and smaller during day time. (We will discuss abnormalities later).

Animals change the etheric sheath considerably when they are active, pleased, frightened etc. Such changes obviously occur also on the level of the greater energy field which is known as the Aura.

The etheric sheath can contract when extreme fear is experienced or expand when a very relaxed state is achieved. Actually, divers and pilots extend their etheric sheath so as to be able to measure the size of their conveyance; this can in the learning stages be very tiring. Some people are good at this but others are not so capable.

Fig. 3.8A
An energy field before it anchors into the physical.

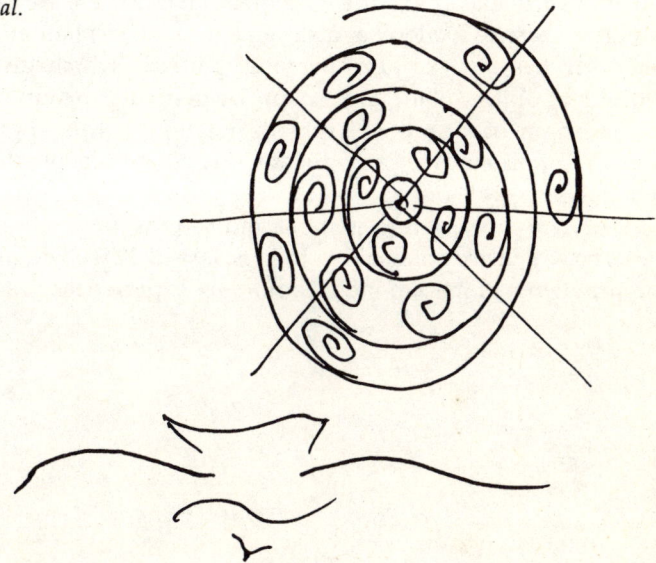

Faults and Problems

In order to grow we have to learn and learning always proceeds via the experiences of how not to do it, in other words we make creative mistakes. (As long as we do not know and we are seekers on the way to understanding, all our mistakes are teaching which become creative. Many famous people actually have found new ideas by having made a 'mistake'). When however, we do know and we let mistakes go by out of slackness and or even deliberately not care about it then they become destructive mistakes. (The worst thing that can happen is to use knowledge and use mistakes to control others, which leads to what one could call sin, guilt or even worse black magic).

Let us go back to the innocent, those who are learning; we are all learning otherwise we would become like stone and worse. There is no master who is not a student and no student who is not also a master.

What we think (especially such thoughts as we pursue regularly for weeks, months, even years) will become built-in patterns in our Aura field. So we are fascinated by mathematics and numbers, we are musicians, or physicists; then we build into this Aura certain patterns which blend harmoniously with out own particular energy field, (remember that there are general patterns because we look at a stone, a mineral, a plant etc., but each one has also its very personal patterns which give the individual object, plant, and so on, its particular beauty.)

The origin of a fault or problem lies within this approach. Food, alcohol, smoking, medicines can all be responsible for changes.

There are now a few general indications for recognising patterns which are not healthy. In Figs 3.9 to 3.12 we will discuss the problems which are most commonly experienced.

This Field of Colour and Patterns – The Aura

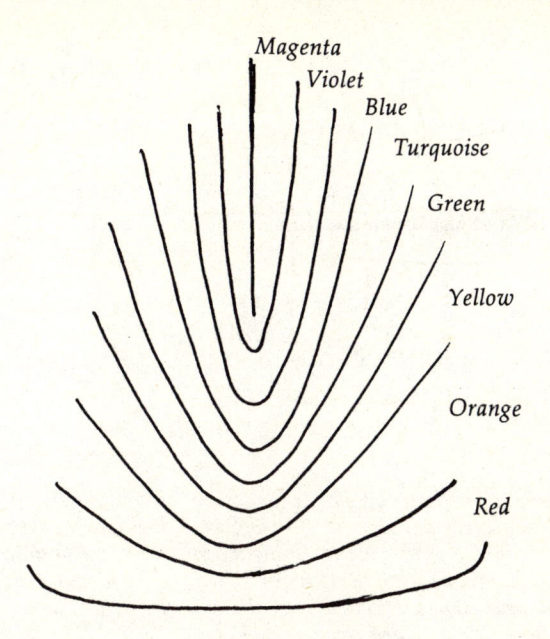

Magenta
Violet
Blue
Turquoise
Green
Yellow
Orange
Red

Fig. 3.9
A child's Aura up to the age of approximately twelve years.

Fig. 3.10
In-coming energy is mentally, in our thought patterns, not accepted – such as in many women who have passed the menopause; they neglect their bodies (mainly breasts and the sex organs); the rejuvenating energy is not able to come into the tissue and a paralysis sets in, eventually this creates such problems as cancer, paralysis, inactivity of the organ etc. Those who are aware of the Aura patterns can see grey, brown, muddy unclear spots in the Aura because the energy can no longer flow and becomes stale.

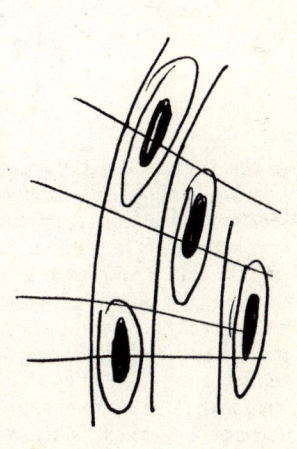

Form, Sound, Colour and Healing

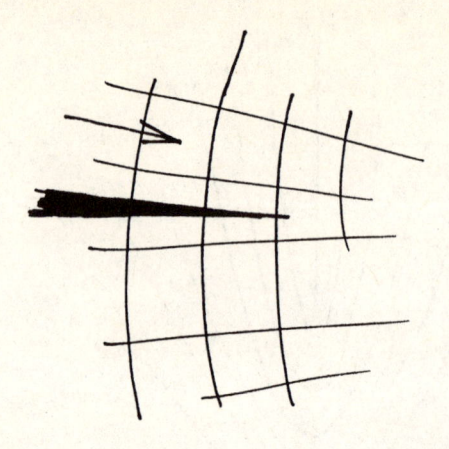

Fig. 3.11

In the vertical energy patterns appear sections like wedges which are 'not there', missing; neither the patterns nor the colours are there; we could call it black. This is very often a serious matter brought on by the use of very strong drugs, especially heroin, acid etc. Eventually there will be so many 'holes', wedges, cut out that the life which was there is dwindling away and eventually the point of no return can be reached.

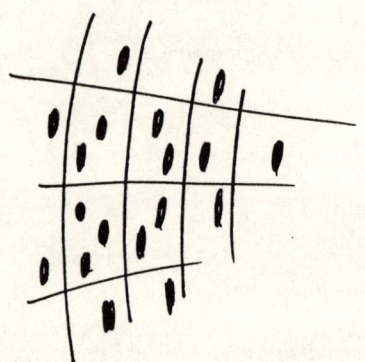

Fig. 3.12

In the horizontal patterns appear flecks, clouds, shadows which are lying there in horizontal form; mostly caused by alcohol, smoking and taking in food which contains light toxins. If we keep watch over this and control drink and toxic foods usually no harm is done, as the vertical energies can very quickly within four hours disperse these shadows and clean out the Aura. If however, the intake grows, say alcohol is used more and more, there will appear a cloudy, murky shadow all over the Aura when all colours become greyish and unclear. Certain illnesses can make these energy patterns so weak that they are just too weak to sustain the physical body. People who suffer tiredness, have a strong desire to sleep all the time, are usually those whose Aura is very much 'watered down', weak and faint.

This Field of Colour and Patterns – The Aura

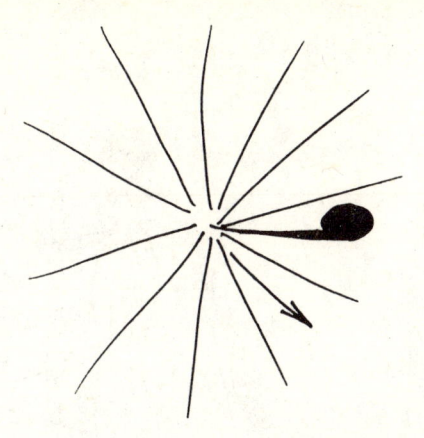

Fig. 3.13
There are always complimentary problems. If as in Fig. 3.9 the body cannot accept the energy, there will be a growing weakness as a result in the body. Here, however, we have to do with a kind of opposite picture. The body stores the energies which should normally be released and thus inflammations and/or swellings of tissue may be the result.

Colour and the Energy Patterns

This is a vast field and in general we can only say that here we have to work on many, many levels.

From childhood to maturity the colours change. The order is: Red, Orange, Yellow, Green, Turquoise, Blue, Violet, Magenta, White Gold; in this order the overall main hue of Colour will go through the nine ages of man's maturing.

Generally there is a slowing down of these colour changes as we grow so that the White Gold is the stage of the Prophet who is asleep in all people to wake and become active at the right moments.

The completed images of colour when total divinity is achieved are the almost White Magenta with a purest Violet, on an indigo blue background.

A whole book would not suffice to describe the intimate complexity and individual colour coding and so we have to leave this chapter for the time being.

All the colours are luminous, shining and a little like the after image colours which we can see when we look at a colour in good light.

Form, Sound, Colour and Healing

THE CHAKRA SYSTEM

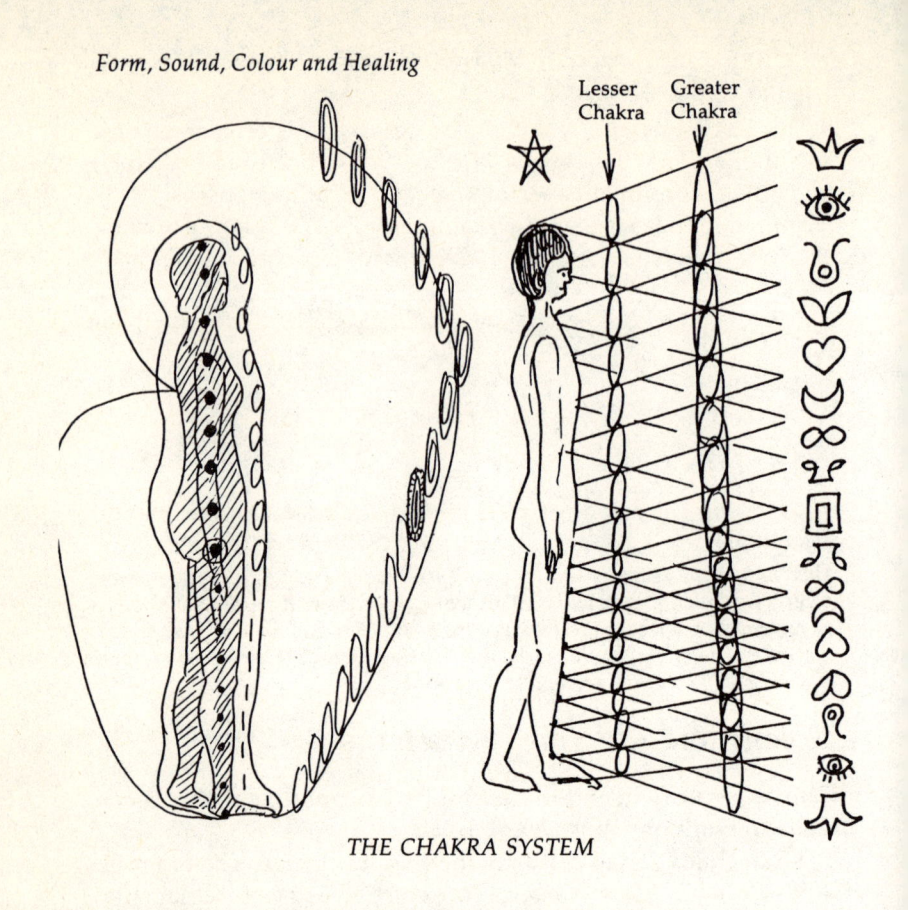

The Chakra System in Relation to the Aura

The Etheric Sheath and the Endocrine System in the Human Body

As the Western human being has developed the intellect, the logic and reasons, so he has also taken hold of the powerful material world. Technology, engineering and all scientific explorations are due to this very decisive step, taking the earth and making our 'modern world' with it's architecture, transport and machinery a viable reality.

This has been done, and in the process the Western person has lost the original visions of the subtle, delicate and mainly invisible environments surrounding all incarnate bodies.

From minerals via plants and animals to the very being of man all things which we cause, weigh and measure, count and experience with our five senses are there because before the present state there were, and still are energies which have helped to create this object, and these energies still support the present existence of these with a kind of cloak or sheath around them. Just as the human skin has seven layers one on top of the other, so also beyond the visible forms are the etheric sheath, the Aura and the global vibratory energies which are the three invisible cloaks around each body that is on this, or for that matter on any other star, only measured in a different substance, other energy and orders.

Through this vibratory field all things are not only linked in one harmonious whole, but all things, yes all, can also be individually contacted.

Western man has problems! Yes, this being has paid for the technical achievements and advantages with a large part of his extra-sensory perception levels.

Maybe we call the third world poor, we look down upon them with a mixture of guilt, charity, pity, etc., but if we looked carefully and had the necessary language to communicate, most of us would be in for a big surprise. Some of those who go with the intentions of getting to know the people of the East and are prepared to listen and look in order to hear and see, find an age old beautiful wisdom and a natural gift of perceiving Auras and the etheric sheath; we find too that they, the people of the East, have still kept the old hearing of the music of the spheres to a large extent. The Eastern person has retained the gifts of the spiritual worlds which stand next to, and around the visible world often even penetrating this material space. Maybe they have kept for us the ancient clairvoyant images, so that we can now, as we begin to feel the loss and crave for the new 'wisdom' go there with a new perception gained in the West and learn, translate, renew or even resurrect this ancient knowledge. Maybe we can thereby make a new beginning built upon the old. Have we not progressed as humanity by keeping one foot on the old stepping stone until we have firmly established our hold on the new place? Maybe by this 'dance' we begin to value what the Eastern person has done for us.

What do we find in the East when we now look for the finer spiritual bodies, the chakras, Aura and the music of the spheres? Did Shakespeare still know about it? A being who made a bridge with his writings to tide us over from the previous state of consciousness to the new one just about to open before our extended senses?

Those of us in the Western world who now open up to the sense which allow us to 'see' again these finer vibrations, will discover these in a very carefully guided way.

The natural path is not a fast or sudden change in our perceptions, but is like a gentle dawn. The student of these faculties will according to his/her present state of awareness, be introduced in as many different ways as there are students in number, but from a certain moment, on the upwards path there will be more and more principles which fit into a generally found pattern. We are mainly two groups of students, one group is biased on the audio vibrations, with these they open up first to a 'new' sphere of sound.

The true student will know that the master being is only the other half of the student, and both these beings in one can identify, clearly and absolutely objectively, the states of their consciousness by knowing always the differences between the clairaudient state and that of a confused mind.

This is also true of the other being who attains clairvoyance. There is a clear and absolute awareness that can tell the true state of expanded consciousness from the:

- Castle in the air day dream.
- Hallucination, when things go wrong in the alignment of the mind and soul.
- The deliberate opening of the third eye or the pituitary to see through and beyond the pure material world.

Both the clairvoyant and the clairaudient state can overlap and be experienced by one individual, either at separate times or combined. The general tendency however, is that one or the other state becomes dominating in an individual person.

First there is perceived the world of pure form and the world of sound, then the whole beautiful kingdom of colour. Colour and form in movement create the state of the master/student who observes the Aura.

The Aura, the three dimensional orb of light, form and colour around all things culminates in its perfection and beauty in the aura of the human form. The main structure is given as a principle whereby all human beings on earth are identified through this unique Aura, regardless of their race, creed, etc. Into this is built the individual structure of a race then the clan, tribe or culture group; right into the closer family, and then the individuality, the soul, the person, who has a unique Aura. But we find over and above that the aforesaid principle always bears an individual imprint in this sacred form however significant variations appear even if only very small. The Colour and Form sequences, the patterns are described in the book "Healing Through Colour" by the Author (C.W. Daniel 1980).

From the galactic space the individual contracts into the earth orb, so on one level all human souls are in contact with each other and live in the same divine space; this is the actual reason why each human or any other form can be located, however far away on this planet. (It is not yet known whether we can actually locate such beings (who do exist outside this planet's vibratory field). However, by using the energy of the dowser there is nothing which needs to remain hidden from the experienced master-student. The question here remains always: "Why and in what state of consciousness do we enquire into this field?" To make contact with anyone in this divine space you must have a real purpose, such as being asked to help, asked to communicate, to counsel. In that moment a step is taken to link two souls more closely. For the purpose of healing such links are permitted. The healer who perceives this Aura, looking into the energy field of another soul, is a privileged individual. Out of the many wonderful encounters on this level I have experienced the most amazing beauty and coloured structures.

The human aura is an orb of colours and a form structure which normally extends to the size of the outstretched arms all round the human body. There is a much less dense large funnel which finally meets between the shoulder blades at the 5th Thoracic vertebrae (the heart); it opens up as it is perceived farther away from the physical body. Although this funnel principle occurs over and over again, as we shall see; it is in this

Form, Sound, Colour and Healing

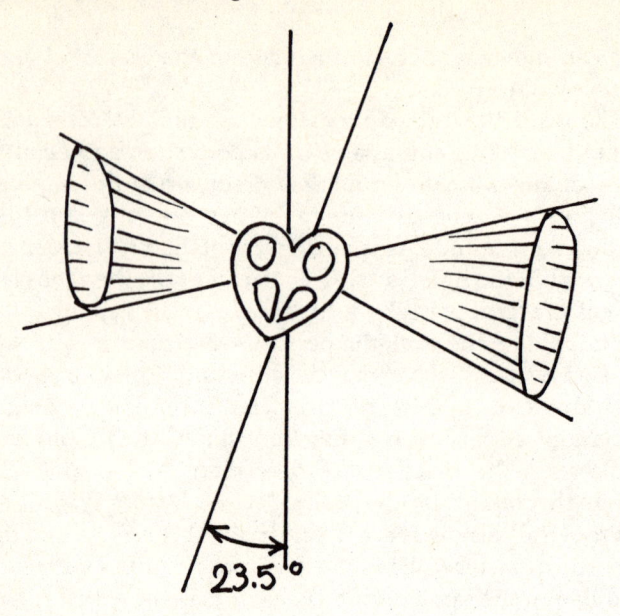

23.5°

place uniquely open and acts as the gateway for the human intention, the path of destiny, the chosen way we go, unless the self-willed ego interferes with this, (which quite often it does to teach us more consciousness). In other words, the ego shows us the limits that lead into cul-de-sacs so that we experience the true middle path, to which we always return.

The Aura is like a three dimensional fan and has as its directives to the manifested human body the chakra systems. All these chakras are a kind of funnelled energy rays which contract onto the actual organ or ductless gland. There are an amazing number of these all over the physical body, opening out as chakras into many directions, However, the human being is a purposeful and guided entity and therefore has a predominant direction which is followed and very clearly marked out when one can observe the awe inspiring order in which this beautiful energy actually co-operates with the health and intentions of will in each moment of an individuality. Each ductless gland has two discs which stand at definite distances from the body. The funnel meets at a point where the rays of energy contract like a pinhole camera and this is at the centre of each physical gland. About three and a half inches away from the body surface we can experience an individual disc about three to four inches in diameter. These stand separated from each other one above the other just where the etheric sheath comes to an end and where the Aura as such starts. There are seventeen main discs from the crown to the soles of the feet. What we observe is that the order is in a clear vertical line all down the body in normal health states. (About abnormal states we will talk later ... in abnormal states of health many distortions and confused patterns occur, colours are murky, faint or too strong). These discs may just border on each other but do not merge into each other at that point.

When we perceive the outer edge of the Aura, then we come to 'see' an amazing and most wonderful structure. Now the funnels do merge and in the normal state there appears this sacred geometrical order of the discs now inter-linking on each others centres so that one centre has two peripheries converging through it. (It is the delight of children when they first discover the art of using a compass to find that six identical circles will merge on a centre point of the seventh circle first drawn).

To the astonishment of the clairvoyant observer the chakra system does not end with the sacral gland; there are most delicate but very pure energies in disc form like a mirror picture right down to the soles of the feet. The pre-structure of an individual is not only going down from the sacral centre (Chakra) but has an incredibly fine order of structures light above the crown, like a filigree sculpture of pure energy. This can become strengthened in people who work on the spiritual self and is like an angelic wing? crown??

What is coming into being on those nine main ductless glands, when the energies touch the periphery of the Aura, is a beautiful tree, the tree of life; that is what the Qabalah teachers find in the tree. Only it seems now that this order has no actual beginning above and no end below. Yet the seventeen discs, which create the actual organs, are quite clearly stated. One amazing thing is that the disc, (which is actually the greater chakra, as apart from the lesser at the three and a half inches distance, where it is inscribed into the last sheath of the etheric energy), that disc which is over the sacral gland is always duplicated and therefore appears to be doubly strong. It actually shows that there are eighteen chakras, two covering the same centre.

When we ask why this is so, we find the answer lies in the fact

Form, Sound, Colour and Healing

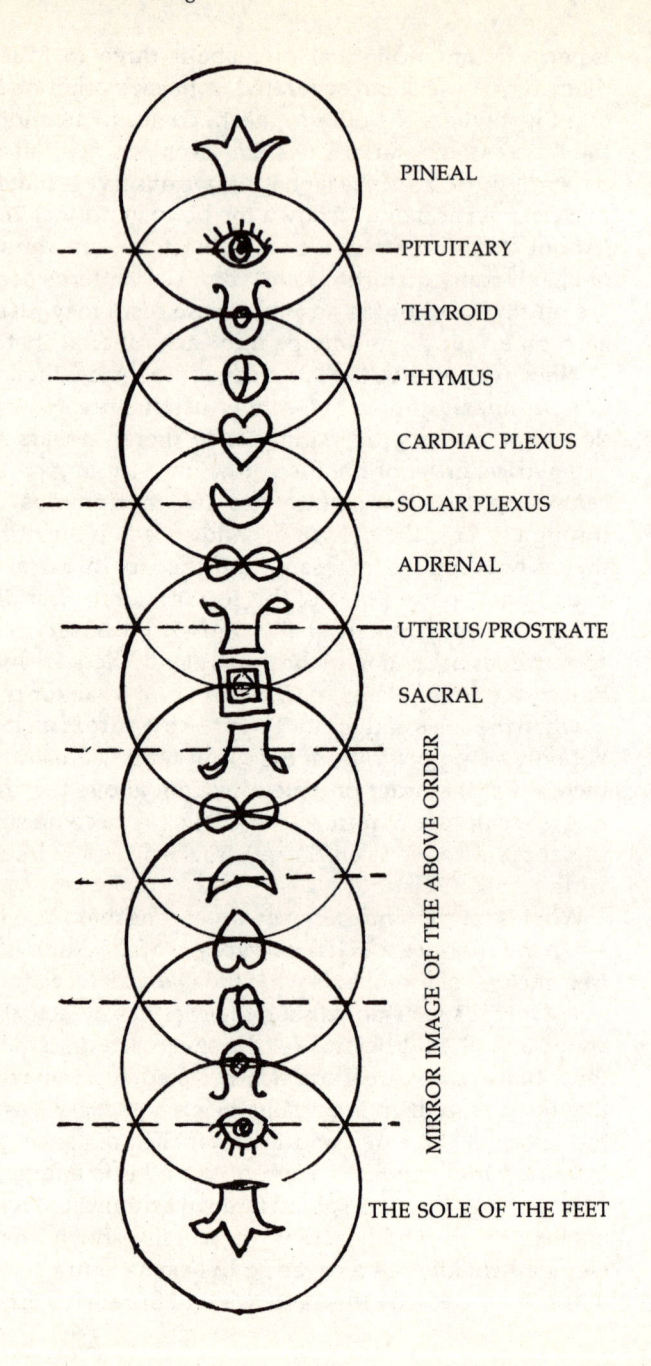

- PINEAL
- PITUITARY
- THYROID
- THYMUS
- CARDIAC PLEXUS
- SOLAR PLEXUS
- ADRENAL
- UTERUS/PROSTRATE
- SACRAL

MIRROR IMAGE OF THE ABOVE ORDER

THE SOLE OF THE FEET

This Field of Colour and Patterns – The Aura

that the physically incarnated human being has there the strongest point, which in the male is creating the female aspiration and thereby the attraction to the opposite sex, and in the female is the male energy to draw to the male being. Thus as the being is physically visible the chakra energies hold there the powerful energy to pro-create and to link up with him or her.

In the usual way when all is comparatively in order and only minor adjustments are made so as to keep the living balances intact, these chakras turn gently in an anti-clockwise direction. In a state of real meditation they can actually be so centred that a gently balancing movement is experienced; standing still is not in my experience.

On the other hand when the physical and sexual approach is made in the foreplay and the moment of accepting and giving, receiving and enjoyment of lovemaking, the heart chakra seems to come very close to the point of standing still. The solar plexus starts to spin gently clockwise, adrenals a little faster, uterus/prostrate quite fast and sacral very fast clockwise. This chakra movement is of course mirrored below in the above described reflected chakra system. When there is a true lovemaking and it is a real communicaton between souls, then the higher chakras are also most beautifully 'dancing'.

When both partners are in harmony this offers a most desirable state of arousal and the culmination in the orgasm should make both return to that state of the very slow balance like the heart chakra; this can last for an indeterminate time and depends on the peace which both partners are prepared to let flow through their bodies; when the man goes to sleep and the women is not brought to her climax then the uncertain spin in the lower chakra areas produce a deep loneliness in the woman which can be very depressing for her. However, even if she has not come to her climax and the man remains awake, gently caressing her and kissing, talking, playing, she will find that chakra balance returning to the usual state and she will not suffer depression.

The spinning of the chakras can often offer an insight into the health picture of an individual person. Some people spin faster than others, this can lead to over stimulation and even neurotic conditions. Quite frequently either one or the other partner can compensate if they are sympathetic towards each other.

Now to the colours. Each chakra has its own dominant colour, but like beautiful flowers, all other spectrum colours are supporting the main colour, and there to shine through the Blue, Violet, Orange or any other colour.

The quality of colour in either pigment or in light is determined really by the factor of how many of the spectrum colours are supporting the actual colour. We can therefore make the picture where the King and the Queen are supported by their entourage.

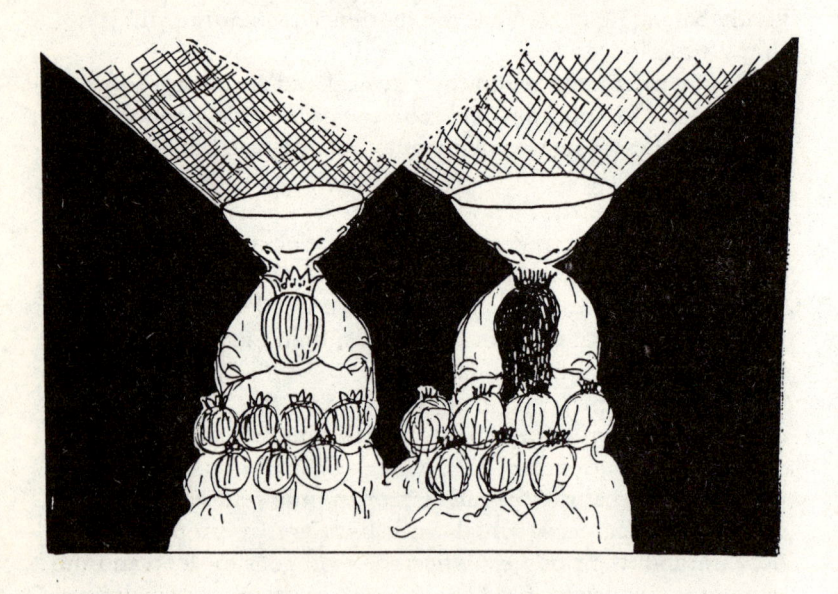

Our visible environment always consists of the two main natures of colour. One is the light and the other is the pigment colour (darkness). The light is known as the subtractive range and the darkness colour as the additive side of colour (pigment). Thus we can say, that what we see is the result of the interplay of both these qualities of colour.

We must therefore ask: Where in-between those amazing principles is the world of colour? It is on that level neither in the one nor in the other but seems to be created as the quintessence of both in cooperation.

The general order is the law of the spectrum; it starts with the strong vital red in the sacral gland where it is a kind of scarlet colour and then ascends as follows:

Red	(Uterus/Prostrate)
Orange	(Adrenals/Kidneys)
Yellow	(Solar Plexus)
Green	(Heart)
Turquoise green	(Thymus)
Turqoise blue	(Thyroid)
Blue indigo	(Pituitary)
Violet	(Pineal)
Magenta	(Pre-manifested/Pure Spirit)

This order is not cancelling any previous orders but over laying this with a further vision.

The different orders of colours and structure in the Aura are depending on the both momentary, temporary or special need of the individual.

The permanent order of any human being on earth is the clear, complete spectrum always. This can be very overpowered by the present need so it may hide the permanent order.

The last mentioned colour "Magenta" is really not any longer focusing on any physical gland but is a very fine thread like beam which opens up most beautifully and very delicately when puberty is completed; usually in a woman this happens much sooner after puberty than with a man. It suggests that in one way or another the man has to come to this later; also it is much hindered by the general level of our present age education. It seems hard to let the spiritual energies be acknowledged when one is seen as the logical, reasonable and intelligent male who conducts the business of this planet, (or does he really?).

There was a culture and no doubt it will come back on a higher level of recognition and consciousness, when the woman lovingly intuitively guided mankind and the male was the co-operator, the complementary being, not subordinate, not a slave, but both stood as master-servants to the great spirit.

There was complete harmony of the colours in the blending of the two beings, it was still there in 500 B.C. and gradually took on the form of powerful domination by the male, who now needs to accept again her most loving protective and wise mother-woman care that does not ever dominate when in a true balance. She is

Form, Sound, Colour and Healing

endowed with an over layer of the blue colour over the whole of her Aura; just as he has the red overlayer over his Aura.

The three bodies of Man

PHYSICAL (shaded): Endocrean system in dots; large ones are the nine main ductless glands, the small dots down to the feet are the shadow or mirror image.
ETHERIC OUTLINE: with lesser chakra discs.
AURA: the large outline with the greater chakra system.

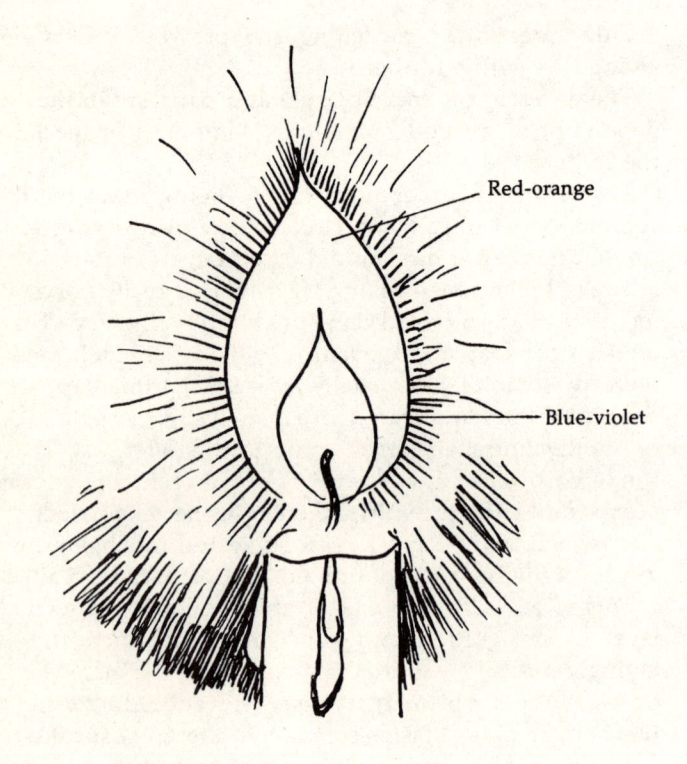

This Field of Colour and Patterns – The Aura

Colour and Your Dress for Health

Although it is not really possible to summarise and make a generall statement it is here attempted to give a lead as to the overall effects colour and dress in male and female can have on the health pattern of most people. It must be born in mind that there are always exceptions to the rule and a chance to add to the given table.

When everything is said and done, this is a working book and wishes to allow the reader to find some of his, her own aspects in this field of colour.

In dress design we can use colours which are chosen and if set in the fashion suggested here the following effects will occur; (all dark areas 'A' are a chosen colour, all 'B' areas (white) will react accordingly to the eye's movements like our Eye Strengthening Chart, see page 107), the lighter the chosen colour the more saturated will appear in the B spaces the complementary colour. The hues will change according to light levels such as daylight, bright, dull or artificial light which comes in many hues and can vary so much from place to place. It is also possible to use B as black and the chosen colour will then play over onto the black with its complementary colour. This could become an exciting new idea in dress design.

Form, Sound, Colour and Healing

DRESS FOR HEALTH	COLOUR	PSYCHOLOGICAL	PHYSIOLOGICAL
Lethargic person with lack of vitality, but well in health. Need or want to be seen. Bad for those who easily tire. Commanding attention.	RED/Green*	Stimulating. Exciting. Pleasure. Alive. Activating	Inhaling. Inner tension to a degree of restriction, ending with exhaustion.
Joyful and for people in need of joy. Anti-depressive, slightly detached and on the light mood. Not for those who need to be in authority.	ORANGE/Blue*	Joyful. Lightness. Release. Pleasure.	Ease in body. Relaxing of seriousness in thinking. Non-involvement.
Detachment from environment. Non-involvement. Good for those who want to be alone and can be alone. Slightly unstabilising and insecure.	YELLOW/Violet*	Detachment. Loss of reason and direction. Spacelessness. Loss of anchorage	Shallow breathing. Irritable. Severing thought from action.
For those who are hyperactive, or need to be very active, but wish not to be involved. Clear judgement. It offers no support nor takes away energy.	GREEN/Red*	Arresting movement. Holding Static. Balance. State of indecision	Minimum liveliness. Held in place. Physical equilibrium.
A good support for people who are easily involved. Calming to nervous tensions. Non-dominating. Fresh and young appearance.	TURQUOISE/Deep Orange*	Cooling. Spacious. Feeling fresh. New.	Pressure releasing. Controlled exhaling, towards release.
Quiet and settled, in control, and to the wearer a relaxing dress. Lets others come near. Lively person receives calm and offers peace.	BLUE/ORANGE*	Relaxing. Unwinding. Feeling of space.	Exhaling, relaxing of tension. Recharging energy to body.
Peace and love involvement without anxiety. Concern not worry. Authority without demand. Meditation and prayer. Good for balance and concentration.	VIOLET/YELLOW*	Inner balance. Reverence. Silence. Peacefulness. Individuality enhancing.	Calming of body. Balance of mind.
Royal and festive dress. In command but without demanding it. Only few can wear it often. Raising of energy level if not conscious enough.	MAGENTA/TURQUOISE*	Stimulating, but lifting into richness of self. Royal awareness.	Individuality underlined composure. A feeling of dignity. Self respect.

* The colours that are named below the actual main colour are the complementary colours.
*1 Colours in order of preferred quantity as found in research. "An investigation into colour concepts in relation to form." 1971. Theo Gimbel. Hygeia Publication, Brook House, Avening, Tetbury, England.

This Field of Colour and Patterns – The Aura

PIGMENT	ILLUMINATION	BEST USE	BAD USE	FORM SUPPORT	USE
Reducing space. Oppressive when dense and strong.	Green objects turn black, generating heat. Dominates other colours.	Dancing. Passage. Enhances activity. Result exhaustion.	Bedrooms. Offices. Stress areas.	All uprights – reducing height or increasing alertness.	(7)[*1] 8%
Space balanced but not restricted. Slightly reducing.	Mellows other colours towards brown; can be sickly and stifling.	Entertainment. Dining area. Passages.	Bedrooms. Study rooms. Stress areas.	Reducing, starkness of space. Creating buoyancy. Loss of anchor.	(4)[*1] 33%
Space lost. Taking away imitation.	Loss of control in work. Some distortion of pigment.	Anti-depressive. Light, mature mind environment.	Offices. Bedrooms. Study & work areas.	Curves. Loops and Waves, movement.	(5)[*1] 8%
Space made static. Dead Lethargic.	Not advisable. Can induce heart palpitations, loss of memory.	Courtyard walls in towns. Operating theatres.	Most living & activity areas.	Waves and horizontal planes.	(6)[*1] 4%
Space free and fresh, but still a holding effect.	Red objects go dark grey. Daylight effect with a slight static influence.	Kitchens. Bathrooms. Some bedrooms & offices.	Activity areas. Play rooms.	Waves. Clouds. Peaks and reducing tall uprights.	(2)[*1] 25%
Enlarging space. The deeper the more relaxing.	Lowest change of pigment in objects. Very relaxing. Space creating effect.	Bedrooms. Office. Treatment & stress areas.	Not actively bad, Dining & entertainment.	Soft wave. Calm horizontals.	(8)[*1] 60%
Awareness of space. Free, yet protected.	Sensuality raised. Inhaling accelerated. Objects change towards dark grey.	Festive areas. Grand-Royal interior.	Hospital ward/ treatment rooms.	Shelter, dome or tent effect. Protection.	(0)[*1] (17%)
Space held in a composed attitude. Controlled feeling.	Good concentration. Reassuring.	Chapels. Entrance halls. Lecture rooms.	Entertainment areas.	The cross, or any strong vertical and horizontal shape.	(3)[*1] 4%

Form, Sound, Colour and Healing

Within Colour Therapy it is always important to realise that there are several colour schemes working in healing thinking. One which is traditional and physical order. Such as:

> Tetrahedron = Red
> Octahedron = Yellow
> Icosahedron = Blue
> Hexahedron = Green
> Pentagon/Dodecahedron = Violet

Using the system on the level of the human integration into life, the order is as follows:

(1) Cosmic conciousness connecting our head with the self, the spirit and the super consciousness;
(2) The mental, ego and thought being the conductor of our order and health;
(3) The emotional astral soul energy spent on making connections with our life;
(4) Next, our metabolic, etheric life system using our nourishment to be health giving;
(5) Lastly our physical-sexual-subconscious being to work here on earth which also entails cell memory and behaviours.

In this order, the five colours are:

(1) Magenta, a very clear luminous colour, going into ultra violet.
(2) Yellow connected with the intellect.
(3) Blue many shaded and many lives.
(4) Green for manifestation of the earthly etheric energies
(5) Red the anchor colour for the physical being. Activity sexuality and going down into the infra-red where the subconscious eneregies are.

Then in both the aura and the spine colours we can find as the norm the full sequence of the spectrum or rainbow order.

When we use the prism as explained in Healing Through Colour we can see two orders, one when we look up to find the colours on the black and white chart with the prism, the other order when we look down to find the colours. Looking up:

Red rises from lower edges.

Violet descends from upper ledges, but reversed when we look down to find the colours.

Magenta and Green in Colour Therapy

All colours have their positive and negative influences, according to how and when they are used.

MAGENTA – The Spiritual colour. It is also the colour most linked to the deep of the night, the colour at the turning point between night and day. It is the colour which is either superconscious or unconscious.

For most of us it is the colour of the unconscious. It is related to the Delta state of brain-wave patterns, and there are very few people on this earth who can maintain consciousness at that deep level. For most of us, it is only reached deep in sleep each night – again it is linked to the middle of the night when even if we are awake, our consciousness is often different from how it is in the day-time.

It is the colour which finds its echo deep, deep down, somewhere deeper within my heart than I can imagine. To go deep within myself in response to this colour means loss of consciousness, losing any sense of who I am and becoming part of a whole.

It is the state of consciousness of the Angelic worlds. Each Angel we perceive as separate, as having a different identity to another – but they are in this state where there is no sense of individuality at all. Each one is the whole; it has no consciousness of 'it's self' or of any separateness. To be in that colour-state is to have no sense of one's separate identity. It is perhaps, the colour of the Mother element of the God – the Darkness, the containing.

Where, then, is the Father?

In the Green.

In the awakening of the world to new life, new promise of growth, as in the Spring-time.

GREEN is LIFE – the colour of life on earth. It is also the colour of human consciousness.

Plants, because they are green in their colour, are very much still existing in the Magenta world. We are magenta on our skin – are we existing in a green world of awareness, of humanness?

Form, Sound, Colour and Healing

Yet it takes the Son to combine the two possibilities, Mother and Father, through His direct experience, through being human, of the Spirit world, otherwise " the light was in the Darkness, and the Darkness recognised it, not".

If we do not 'give off' the magenta hue, but absorb it instead continually, it can be a 'death wish' – a wish to draw back our energy from the 'green' world, and to be no longer conscious – a sinking into unconsciousness. This is the negative experience of Magenta. It can also be made positive especially when a person is dying, as this colour has links with high states of active awareness, – samadli, sartori, many names in many languages.

And green, of course is also in the negative – death. The colour of nature decaying and rotting. Used against cancer it can both attack cancer cells and balance the magenta, giving a person literally an influx of life energy.

Pre-Birth Magenta

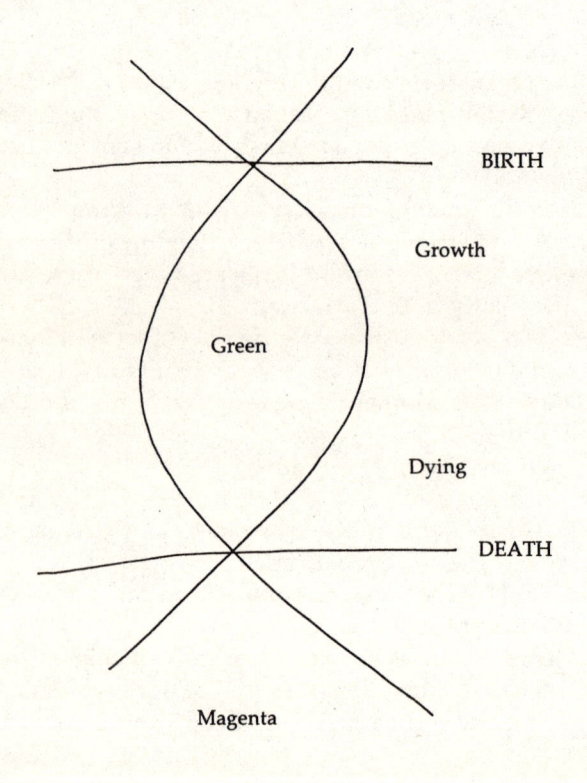

BIRTH

Growth

Green

Dying

DEATH

Magenta

This Field of Colour and Patterns – The Aura

Magenta is the pre-birth colour the embryo's link with the Infinite, where it was, and from which it partly feeds. Birth is the focusing of that Being into a point of inversion, out into the world of green, where it grows until one day it is called back and the pattern repeats in reverse order through the point we call death.

Suppose we were to keep growing and growing?

There can also be other deaths, other births, in one's lifetime. We could live many lives of personality experience in one, if we knew how to, and if this was what we had chosen beforehand. Astrology and Palmistry are two ways that point out if these possibilities are there. Numerology and name-sounds assist the change.

- Speed of sound: 25.000 c. per sec. cannot normally be heard by people. 15,000 to 19,000 can reach human hearing.
- $7.5\ 10^{14}$ = blue/$4.6\ 10^{17}$ = red. We cannot see above blue, nor below red, which is in darkness.
- Growing Plants under Colour (daylight). Hygeia Studio publication 1974.

- The Decent of Eve – Theo Gimbel 1974 also: *Developing Higher Levels of Perception*.
- E. F. Schumacker: *Small is Beautiful* – T. L. C. Factor (Peter Tompkins & Christopher Bird: *The Secret Life of Plants*).

The Five Octaves of the Human Spine

The repetition of five and eight has always been an important configuration; to multiply these two figures we come to the number forty which is a well-known number connected with many aspects of development, both physically and spiritually.

The centre of the human body, the instrument, the tool through which we express ourselves here on earth, can be seen to contain five times eight bones.

The skull has eight bones which are really metamorphosed vertebrae. This octave, in the work of Colour Therapy, is the supreme most luminous colour area, where the colours are so fine that they are frequently almost white. This octave also holds for us the centre into which our thoughts are received. It is the spiritual centre where the self, the super conscious, is present. In our work, using the spine as a diagnostic tool, this area can only be acknowledged as being the source of our motivation here on earth. It stands supreme above and is in the old master paintings frequently recognised as being illuminated when these painters wished to portray angels and saints. It is said that the human face contains what you are, the profile; and what you like to be, the en-face; the eyes are windows to the soul; the whole face portrays the person.

So we take the skull as being the spiritual super conscious part of our client or patient.

First octave	Spirit, Self superconscious	S.S.S.
Second octave:	Mental, ego, thought	M.E.T.

This Field of Colour and Patterns – The Aura

Third octave:	Emotional, astral, soul	E.A.S.
Fourth octave:	Metabolic, etheric, life	M.E.L.
Fifth octave:	Subconscious, physical, sexuality	S.P.S

If we place this into a meaningful order we come to realise that the order is not a ladder but a circle experience. Also, we should notice that the fifth octave stands now in direct contact with the first so that there is an important link between spirituality and sexuality.

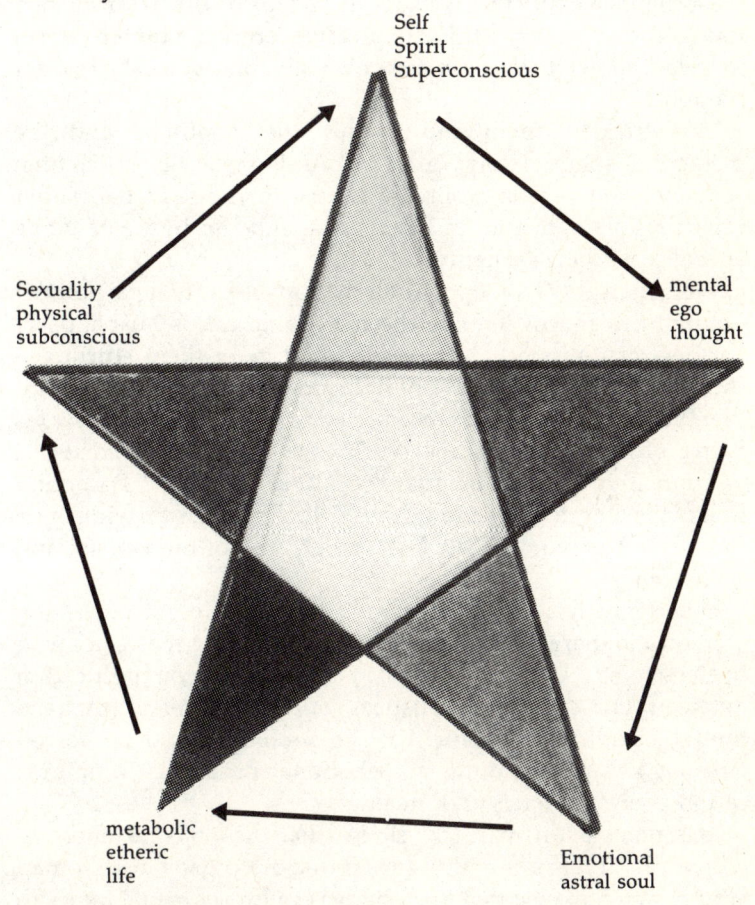

Fig. 3.14 see colour page (ix)

In our work, which always commences with counselling our client, we regard this above picture of a human person's make-up as very important. He/she is, above all, a spiritual person whose invisible, divine aspect is with him/her to a greater or lesser degree. What we need to do is to make a new picture of this person, which in every state of not well-being is diminished. We look at the illness as a teaching to the person. A teaching over which this person can be taught to become a better conductor. In other words, the pictures which we have about our own person must be 'renovated', brought back to a state of wholeness. In most clients we find that we have at first to do with a diminished image, that they do not think in positive terms and thereby have, in a way, allowed some diminished health patterns to be in their thoughts.

This trickles down and colours the emotional and the metabolic aspects finally expressing itself physically which then separates the person from the return to the spiritual, super conscious state. It also, in most cases, ends up in the negative appraisal of their sexuality.

Women mostly look upon their menopause as being a point of 'dying', the end of their fertile lives, and unless husbands or partners can support them, praise and carry them spiritually through this time, there is often the danger that they look upon their bodies, breasts and reproductive organs, their sexuality, as being now 'over and done with'. Such negativity creates a vacuum first in their mental, then their emotional state, and finally the etheric – life energy fades. Such women are wide open to let into this void space, cells which are not humanised and called cancer.

Experience has taught that we can counsel eight out of ten women and thereby avoid any operations such as mastectomy or hysterectomy. Ideally, if there was enough communication between the superconsciousness of a person and the ego thought/mental, then much of the problem could be solved already, before becoming an emotional problem. Communication is eighty per cent of healing.

It is not known in many circles that the physical energies which fill the breasts and the reproductive organs in a woman after the menopause make room for very fine spiritual forces to work through these organs. Therefore, a grandmother can give to

This Field of Colour and Patterns – The Aura

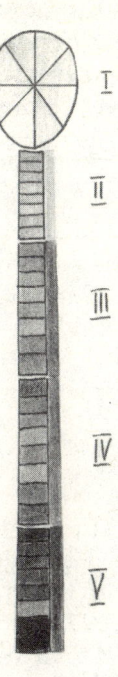

Fig. 3.15 see colour page (x)

her grandchildren an energy which the mother has, as yet, not available. It also happens to the male, the Grandfather; a maturer mind, and a deeper spirituality flows through these, 'wise' human beings.

This does not mean that physical communications have to recede. Love making is simply on another, more mature level, and filled with a new quality which does not come through the young bodies, instruments. Quite often one can see in older people that the aura has a golden layer of light with this almost white magenta colour. The education of this age to help us to become, in all respects, dignified human beings, is still very scantily available and we should be very anxious to bring such knowledge to more and more people. This subject* in the book: *The Gospel of Joy and Communication* is enlarged upon.

The first octave of colours, the skull is like the heart in man, a bridge to connect the spiritual cosmic superconscious to the Ego,

*Hygeia publication 1980, Theophilus Heliodor

the mental thought world. The Skull we call Octave I, now we proceed through the remaining four Octaves to complete the circle. It is vital that we see our own being as a whole. There is the higher, almost white, magenta representative of the Spirit.

The yellow, the mental area, the thinking, II;
The blue pertaining to our astral the soul, III.

Coming down further and more to grips with our body functions we experience the metabolic etheric life energies in Green IV and return towards the spiritual world through the colour of physical energy – red V, making a bridge to the spirit.

The next section of this chapter must be understood to be adhering to the following order when these colours appear in the charts of a client. (Patient).

Octave I. The eight colours in almost white luminous state are almost not there. See Fig. 2/3 (the old master painters would use a golden halo around the head of angels and saints). This is our skull composed of eight bones which are like flower petals each a metamorphosed vertebrae. We must also remember that this is the part of our body which is used to bring into this physical life the ideas of the invisible world, the spiritual cosmic energies; also the Divine Kingdom. Recall this Octave I in connection with all the now following colours.

Octave I the skull is not considered for therapy but through it stream the spiritual essences into the Mental, Ego Thought which is covered by the next octave.

Octave II is the mental–ego–thinking area, human Kingdom.

Octave III represents the emotional–Astral soul–animal Kingdom.

Octave IV influences our metabolic–etheric and life body. Plant Kingdom.

Octave V is the subconscious–will–physical body. Mineral Kingdom.

Magenta: is interpreted as being the quality to dissolve–let go of and overcome.

Violet: is the energy of dignity—self respect and maturity

Blue: the quality to relax—expand—and peace.

Turquoise: Purity—freshness—cleansing.

The more feminine colours, mentioned above, are used in counselling as linking man more to the spiritual state.

The following colours are more of the masculine, earth levels. However, the green represents a 'bridge state' to 'link the spiritual' in man to the physical.

Green: Equilibrium—Neutral—Balance

Yellow: Detachment—intellect.

This colour becomes a very unacceptable pigment in schizophrenia. Violet would be a healing colour in such conditions.

Orange: Joy – movement – gentle energy.

Red: Power – physical consciousness, will, sexuality.

MAGENTA
Octave II, Mental, ego, thoughts (Cervical 1 – Thorasic 1)
The need *to dissolve, to move away from, to overcome* nostalgic thinking, making old pictures of the past and thereby avoiding work with the present needs.

Octave III, emotional, astral, soul starting with (Thorasic 2) there, also in the feeling area, is the need to move out of the yesterday, past, images.

Octave IV, metabolic, etheric, life (starting with Thorasic 10) old behavioural patterns are retained. Traditional often not even thought through, just copied from family. Mother or father obedience which does not now apply.

Octave V, subconcious, physical, sexuality (starting with Sacrum 1). Acting out of old memory the subconscious needs to follow a pattern even if it is now no longer useful. Staying in ruts which become compulsory.

Some advise for image making of Magenta:

II: M.E.T. Visualise a very fine, almost white, magenta blossom

Form, Sound, Colour and Healing

above your head into which you can lay all your deep wishes for the release of negative thoughts. It will bear seeds, fruits which will become real in your being and sink through your whole system.

III: E.A.S. Let this image of the blossom sink into your heart so that all is now, and now is important, the magenta has become stronger and includes the love for the 'new' state.

IV: M.E.L. The magenta blossom opens up and includes your present state of the digestive area, think of being filled with the seed of now, the past is not important, it has brought you here where you are.

V: S.P.S. You are sitting in the deep magenta blossom, now the present time is the only time you are really you. Include there also what your sexuality means, its the path through which yesterday, here on earth, was expressed what is possible tomorrow. You are in the now because you are here leading to the Spirit–Self–superconscious – this is with you this very moment.

Violet (skull, Octave I not included) gracious–dignity from the Spirit–Self–superconscious (purple and more royal violet).

Octave II: In the *mental–ego–thought*; this person needs self-respect, acknowledgement to be a worthy person, to be treated and seen with dignity.
  It is this eternal space, now in deeper blue that fills you through the guide who brings peace to you by the lake and the blue sky.

Octave III: the *emotional–astral–soul*; bring into this part of your being the above feeling. Control of negative and unpleasant expressions, hate, anger, uselessness, etc: strengthen love, listen to positive feelings.

Octave IV: the *metabolic–etheric–life*; do not let your lower system become a despised, and even horrible, area. It has often to do with the eating habits and the whole digestive area. Eat in a gracious and thankful way and also offer gratitude for the energies which come into the body through nourishment.

Octave V: the *subconscious–physical–sexual*; bring into this the dignity and grace with which we are endowed.

Violet II: see a gracious person holding out his hands (if you are a woman, or for a homosexual a male) he is dressed in violet, very dignified. He lets you be in his presence where all is beautifully respected as it is now from your state in your thoughts, which are not yet perfect. He guides you into a more perfected state. Accept his hands and go near him as far as you can make the effort, to be enveloped in his cloak of violet (very luminous fine violet). (In the case of a man or a lesbian woman, the figure seen can be a priestess or a female being).

III: she/he writes down with your help the present states of your emotional, inadequate feelings and tells you that because of these you can know the positive; the respectful, the dignified you.

IV: he/she offers you nourishment which is to strengthen your being, the violet is deeper now and your body is being protected by his/her blessing.

V: you are reminded that you should write down in your subconscious, sexual being this colour which can heal you and make you a dignified whole person, allowing the link to be re-established to the self, from the subconscious to the spirit.

You are brought into this world by way of the physical love and the memories which lie deep in your cells link up with the physical life-stream, the whole of dignified sexuality.

Blue I, Spirit–Self–Superconscious – the eternal link to peace – expansion and relaxation.

II: M–E–T. Let there be peace in your Thoughts, work on the levels of relaxation, bringing into this area the thoughts of expansion. Be alert to such moments when your thoughts are invaded by moments of peace and let such moments return and become more often available to you for longer periods through blue.

III: E–A–S. In the area of your chest feel peace and relaxation come in and avoid anxiety and restrictions, recall blue again and again. It is this eternal space, now in deeper blue that fills you through the guide who brings peace to you by the lake and the blue sky.

IV: M.E.L. Fill this area below the heart with expanding

peaceful blue. You are by a blue lake with a clear peaceful sky. 'Your friend' in blue is with you; it can be the Madonna Maria or the Priest, the Godlike Father (depending on your own leanings towards a female or a male being):

Your whole being is enveloped in this slowing down through your anxiety – dissolving blue. Visualise the peaceful blue sky and lake which stretches out expanding its tranquility of peace.

V. The blue is now very deep and peace descends into the whole of the body. Here is a strength which relaxes and pacifies all.

The Guide brings love with this blue peace. It is offered to you and you see yourself taking it. All is well: there is no rush or hurry. Even your cells are now enjoying peace.

Turquoise I: Clear, clean, pure. A very fine sheen of blue–green, green–blue, almost white light, hovers above you, enclosing your head. It is a cooling experience.

II: M.E.T. The mental field is being rested. Any unwanted heat is cooled down. Any inflammatory condition in the area of thinking, and the ego, is now controlled.

Make the picture of a wood in the summer where the green blends with the blue of the sky. You are there. You are also in company (you are never alone: many friends think of you).

III. E.A.S. The turquoise is deeper and its cleansing, cooling, clearing effect is strongly playing into the chest area.

Bring into your emotions and your soul this being who can clear your breathing and let you experience that you drink into you the gift which is offered, like some cool, clear turquoise liquid that refreshes you.

IV: M.E.L. The turquoise is darker now, but still transparent, like all these colours must be. Any inflammatory condition in this part (in all the functions where nourishment energies play a part) there is now through this colour the healing of the body made possible.

The being offers you this chalice, and you are experiencing its beneficial influence.

V: S.P.S. The deep, shining turquoise is now in your whole body, purifying, reducing tensions and making a clear, clean experience happen where before was too much heat. Any inflammatory areas are cleared up, and when there is, perhaps, some eczema, this can be cleared. Women during their period should make contact with turquoise.

See that your communications with the turquoise being is beautiful and absolutely pure. Energies flow where before was not enough health.

Fig. 3.16 see colour page (ix)

Remember that your brain in the last incarnation on earth is now your heart. As you allow yourself to think today you will direct the organ of balance and rhythm for your next life.

The heart is seen as being green and the head as being in this light resembling a white–magenta. (The brighter this magenta is, the deeper the equilibrium colour or complimentary colour green).

Green I: S.S.S. There is a higher, non material heart in absolute balance. You are now below this, you are in it.

II: M.E.T. Balance in thoughts; equilibrium in judgement when making mental appraisals of circumstances and events find a neutral ground to be in. It is the contact colour with the materialised existence. Manifested energy spirit becoming matter.

III: E.A.S. Stabilising emotions, also dissolving, as the green becomes stronger, bio-chemical structures; neutralising, putting into a balance, it is the colour to go through but not to remain in.

IV: M.E.L. Deep green influencing the whole of our nutrition process and the balancing of etheric energies to sustain life often useful in conditions of cancer, visualise green.

V: S.P.S. Very deep green now to put the body into a state from where the subconscious choice can be balanced out by making the preparatory thoughts influenced by the very shining green heart shape. (Let the sexuality be of such that both parties are equally strong, both having the same share of joy acknowledging each other to be different but the scales are in absolute balance.

Yellow I: S.S.S. The light of the earth now shines into this balance state (see the green heart) now shining out with this almost white–gold–yellow. Our physical light here on earth is the reflection of the spiritual–superconscious light.

II: M.E.T. Yellow, the intellect, the energy of detachment, (separation) we must guard our thinking not to judge: "I am in the right!" etc. jealousy, envy, abstract. It can cause quarrels between people if your thoughts are in this detached (non-compassion) state. The yellow, spiritual light is not in a state of judgement, but rather to see by!

III: E.A.S. the yellow is now strong and in this area has some connection with breathing the air, but breathing is also communication, and let the yellow colour not stand in between your conversation between your thoughts and your soul. Rather make it into a bridge, illuminated to allow clarity between all things, first in yourself as a soul being then between all those you meet.

IV: M.E.L. the deeper yellow can now regulate the digestive system and make a better use of the daily food to go as energy to the whole body. Also to sort out the space where things are stuck and even wasted through hanging on to old, useless energies.

Imagine that some being is going through your whole body (specially below the heart) with a lantern and clearing up because that being can now see.

V: S.P.S. shed a deep golden yellow into your subconscious, sexual, physical being and bring into it that detached, yet objective view of yourself; (do not become through it self judgemental). Link yourself back to the area (read Yellow I once more).

Orange I: S.S.S. This freeing colour of joy, do not let it lead you into weakness of self. In this joy, you could become so happy that you would blindly follow whoever takes responsibility on your behalf.

II: M.E.T. Lifting depression in your thinking, bringing lightness and ease to disperse heavy thoughts. Self contentment appears. It is the dancer, the one who also jests and has little care.

III: E.A.S. Orange will lift gloom and brings a kind of openness into your feelings. The colour will make you overcome any heaviness.

IV: M.E.L. The digestive system is re-enlivened and frees energies so that the body is enjoying the nourishment, i.e. what we can transfer from the physical food into the system of our body, freed energies which can lift the body soul and thinking into a state of joy. The thought processes are closely related to the digestive system.

V: S.P.S. Orange in this region is the letting go of all physical concerns, heaviness of the body. It increases sensuality and disperses weight, i.e. slow and lethargic patterns, with its joy it makes every cell want to be free. Often the desire to make love is experienced. It is the evening colour.

Red I: S.S.S. A strong presence of being here, awareness and power.

II: M.E.T. I am important. I am now here, drawing consciousness, and strong energy into my person, stimulating self-importance.

III: E.A.S. Here the red colour is a very powerful, almost overpowering experience, not many can endure it for long. It is really not a colour for the soul because it has the capacity to fix, bind and hold. The soul and emotions in their nature are really always flexible and red binds this flow. It can, in cases of indecisiveness and constant flow, however, for a time help to stabilise and secure to the present.

IV: M.E.L. A speeding up of the life energies often too fast, and too strong. Not all people can stand in this colour for reasons of the powerful effect over their metabolic body. The etheric energies are over vitalised and tiredness can follow which then creates a strong urge to action.

V. S.P.S. Red can create here so much power that it becomes to strong. It can, however, also be helpful where the lack of energy has a paralysing effect. It is the colour to increase sexuality, to see red can lead people, especially men, into such sexual urges that it goes out of control. Men worse than women as their whole nature is already steeped deeper into the area of this colour (denser and masculine power) which dominates strongly the male body.

Form, Sound, Colour and Healing

See now how the whole of our colour being is related downwards and upwards in a stream of changing light, the whole spectrum or rainbow is never ending. We are in the middle stream of it where the colours which have become recognisable out of the ultra violet go through us, keeping us well and descending into the invisible colours of the infra reds. Of course on both ends the colours continue only we do not have the facilities (as yet) to see them. Fig. 4.3.

We should now consider how we can see our fellow men and work on a practical basis with them.

Fig. 3.17 see colour page (xi)

This Field of Colour and Patterns – The Aura

The sunlight is showing different colours of the spectrum according to the angle of the sun in relationship to the Pentagondodecahedron. (The Hexahedron will produce no colours meaning that this solid, representing the earth, is neutral).

Below are two photographs taken first at 10.50 a.m. and again at 13.55 p.m. – mark the shift in the spectral colours.

These spectral photographs show the power of colour. The colours are produced by a crystal 8" in diameter made of clear epoxy resin and cast in the form of a Pentagondodecahedron. The colours are recorded on pure white paper and thus show how very strong they are rendering the paper, in contrast, almost black. A similar crystal but in the form of a Hexahedron will produce no colours at all. Thus angles possess or do not possess refraction capacity. All strong light and darkness edges show to the trained eye a rim of either the red or blue spectrum, even without a prism which simply enlarges the edges. The natural law is: Darkness about light = the ultra violet half and light above darkness = the infra red complementary half.

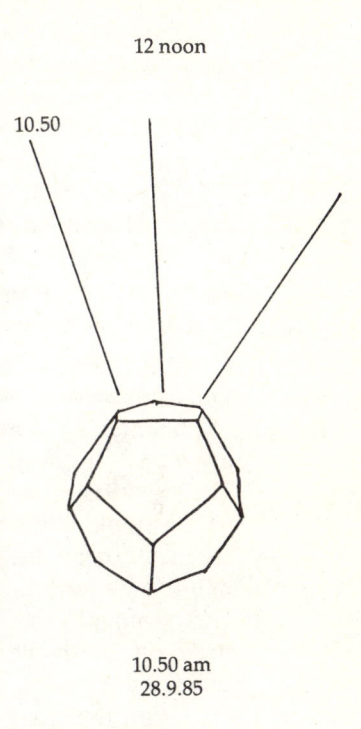

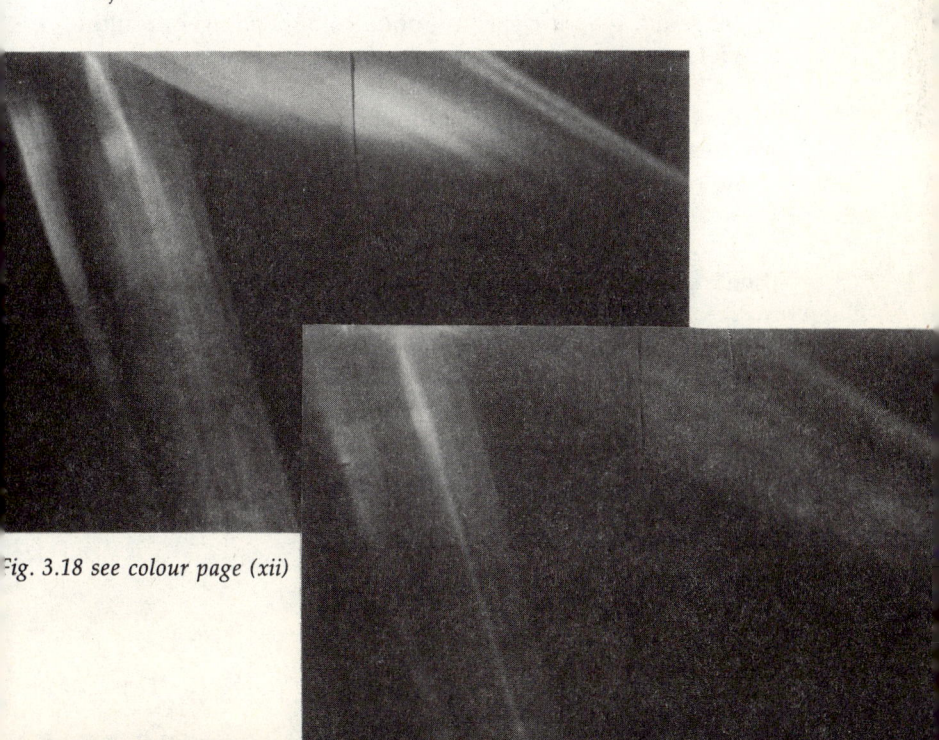

10.50 am
28.9.85

Fig. 3.18 see colour page (xii)

Form, Sound, Colour and Healing

Within Colour Therapy it is always important to realise that there are several colour schemes working in healing thinking.

One which is traditional and physical order. Such as:

    Tetrahedron = Red
    Octahedron = Yellow
    Icosahedron = Blue
    Hexahedron = Green
    Pentagon/Dodecahedron = Violet

Using the system on the level of the human integration into life, the order is as follows:

(1) Cosmic consciousness connecting our head with the self, the spirit and the super consciousness;
(2) The mental, ego and thought being the conductor of our order and health;
(3) The emotional astral soul energy spent on making connections with our life;
(4) Next, our metabolic, etheric life system using our nourishment to be health giving;
(5) Lastly our physical–sexual–subconscious being to work here on earth which also entails cell memory and behaviour.

In this order, the five colours are:

(1) Magenta, a very clear luminous colour, going into ultra violet.
(2) Yellow connected with the intellect.
(3) Blue many shaded and with many lives.
(4) Green for manifestation of the earthly etheric energies.
(5) Red the anchor colour for the physical being. Activity, sexuality and going down into the infra red where the subconscious energies are.

Then in both the aura and the spine colours we can find as the norm the full sequence of the spectrum or rainbow order.

When we use the prism as explained in *Healing Through Colour* we can see two orders, one when we look up to find the colours on the black and white chart with the prism, the other order when we look down to find the colours. Looking up:

Red rises from lower edges.

Violet descends from upper edges, but reversed when we look down to find the colours.

Chapter 4

The Colour Therapy Instrument

A metal housing, stove enamelled blue, unless otherwise instructed, standing in all 5'8" high, 1'4" wide, and 11½" deep.

It is assumed that the Colour Therapist is familiar with the use of this Instrument as far as the actual treatment is concerned.

What is, however, not necessarily the same on each instrument, is the technical layout as we strive to improve all the time the electric section.

The use of it is taught in our courses here at Hygeia Studios. Even if you are not trained with us, it is important to have at least read my book *Healing Through Colour* and know about its content in Chapter 6: Practical Advice on using Colour to treat illness (pp. 121–152). This book can be obtained from us or directly from C.W. Daniel, 1 Church Path, Saffron Walden, Cambridge, England.

When all the cables are connected you may switch on the instrument which is marked 0 for off, and 1 for on. This will fade in the WL (top filter box). This will now be alight for as long as you wish it to be. You can control the illumination level with the first dimmer switch of the three dimmers on the right of the controller face.

Now set your other two light levels. High for cervical 1 to thorasic 1. Medium for thorasic 2 to thorasic 10, and low for thorasic 11 to lumbar 5. When you have set this on the controls replace the wood door with the opening to coincide with the starter button (black 5) which follows the serial lights; then invite your patient to come in. When he/she is fully comfortable – push your starter button and the session is now on its way.

The sequence will last for 19¼ minutes, after which the WL will come on automatically and stay on until your patient has left the treatment room and you switch off by removing the door. All filter and control boxes have rubber feet so they sit safely on each other.

The Connection System

You will have to purchase your own Connector according to your country's regulations. It must have a live, negative and an earth pole. This will be fitted to the long connection cord as follows:

$$\text{Brown} = \text{live}$$
$$\text{Blue} = \text{negative}$$
$$\text{Green/Yellow} = \text{earth}$$

The three filter-boxes are identical and in the building up on top of the control-box you need not pay attention to which is first, second or third.

The Colour Therapy Instrument

In the course of research since 1980 we have slightly altered some of the old ways, we now use craftsman blown Stained Glass instead of our old filters and the time controller has been changed so as to start the complementary colour with 3¼ minutes and not with 5¼ minutes as before. The proportions of treatment colour to complementary colour are thus better adjusted. The reasons for our stained glass are described here and are very important.

The three leads which connect the filter boxes to the Control-box are simply the long one to the working light (WL or W), the medium to the therapy filter box (TL or T) and the very short one from the complementary filter-box (CL or C) to the Control unit marked 'C' – Both ends of these three cables are identical and so again it is not necessary to observe which ends go to the control-box, or to the Filter boxes.

Your plug (connector) to main power is fused with a 5 amp

The Colour Therapy Instrument

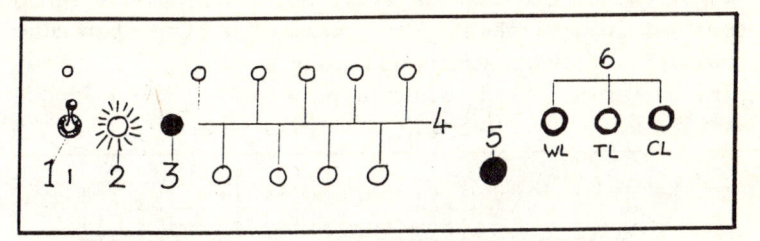

1 = on/off switch
2 = light indicating on/off
3 = Fuse (1 amp)
4 = Sequence indicators
5 = Starter push button
6 = Dimmers

Fig 4.1 Control Panel (at the base of the instrument)

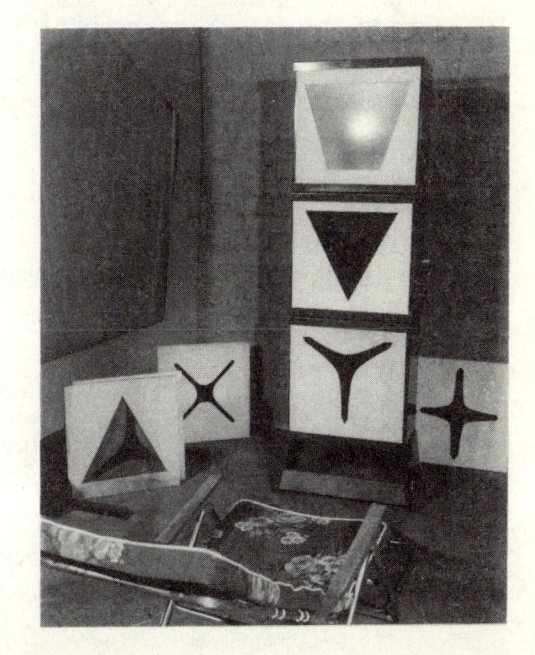

see colour page (xiii)

fuse. However, there is a 1 amp fuse to safeguard the controller fitted and a spare is supplied.

Colours in the filters for the Colour Therapy Instrument

The most outstanding feature of these filters is that the craftsman

Form, Sound, Colour and Healing

blown stained glass has in every one colour a very broad spectrum. In principle this is not measurable by any particular standard, and an analysis is practically worthless.

In our graph (purely illustrative), we show this principle which holds for all our 8 major shades. See Fig. 1.

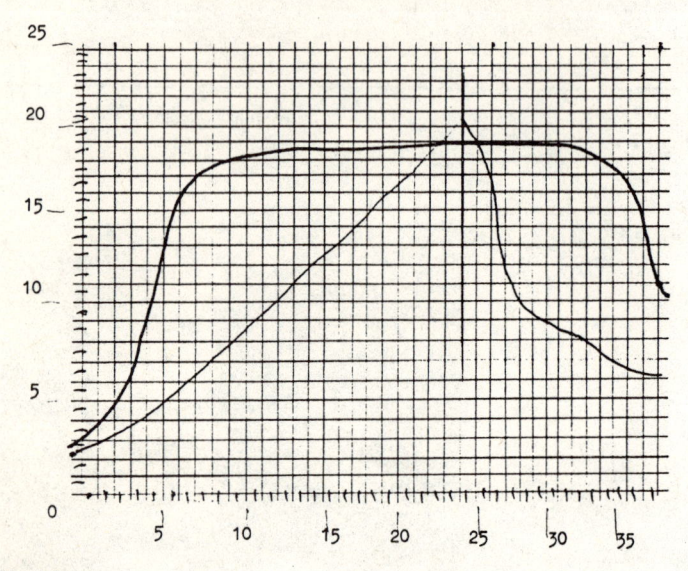

Fig 4.2

Eight is the number of harmony and the number of the clearly differentiated colours in the basic spectrum made up of the following shades, clearly visible with a prism.

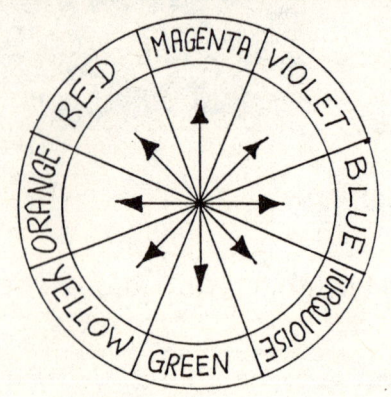

Fig 4.3

The Colour Therapy Instrument

Now the reason for this difficulty in the measurement of the analysis is, that within each of the eight shades are contained all the variants of every one of these hues. This is the glass which was used for ages in the old Cathedrals and the places where stained glass was used for artistic purposes.

If we take any one of these sections as shown in Fig 4.2 the result will look like this:

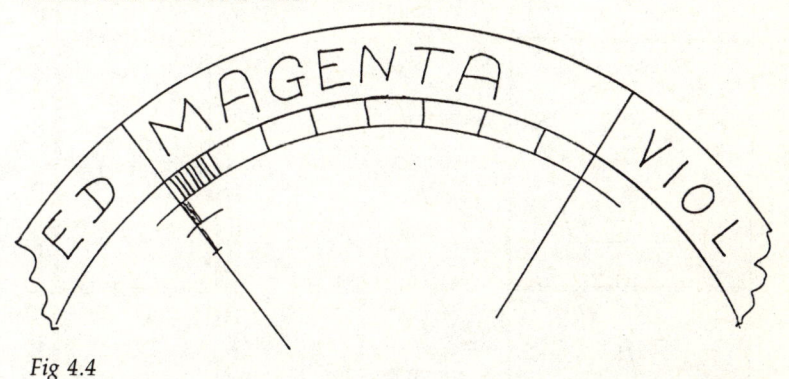

Fig 4.4

The one eighth of the spectrum, as a whole, is now sub-divided into eight sub-magentas, which in turn is sub-divided into eight *ad infinitum*.

$$8 \times 8 = 64 \times 8 = 512 \times 8 = 4096 \times 8 = 32768 \times 8 = 262{,}144 \times 8 = 2097{,}152 \times 8 = 16{,}777{,}216 \times 8 = 134{,}215{,}728$$

(One hundred and thirty-four millions, two hundred and fifteen thousand and seven hundred and twenty-eight) – this astronomical figure for one colour of eight reaches into infinity as colour shades go far beyond human measurements.

We speak about the fact that our own human body is a most accurate and sensitive instrument with which we can measure the impact and effect that any environmental changes have upon it. Above all, there is a very clear indication that the finest degrees of light changes are recorded and reacted upon by the pituitary gland. Looking at the pituitary gland we can call it a filter which receives all incoming colour vibrators, and selects what is now necessary for the person to receive. In Fig. 3.1 you can thereby see the incredible spread of the spectrum of each colour that facilitates the above reaction.

Form, Sound, Colour and Healing

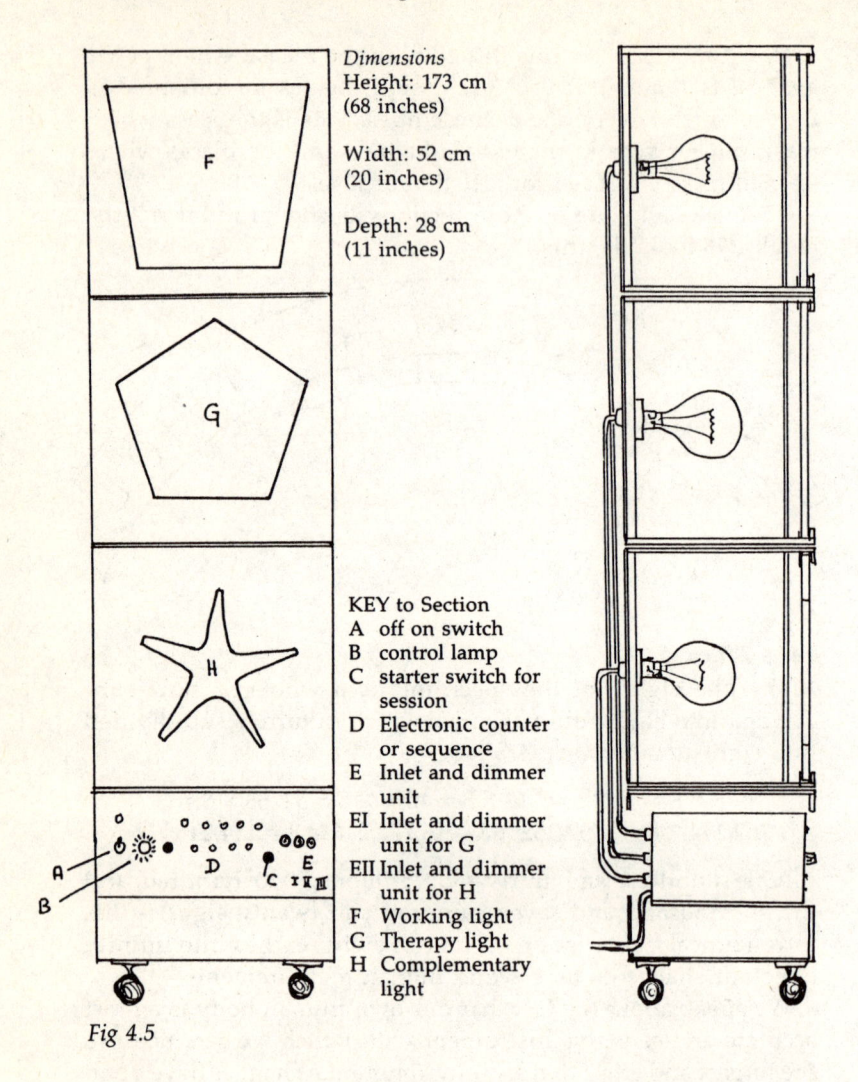

Dimensions
Height: 173 cm
(68 inches)

Width: 52 cm
(20 inches)

Depth: 28 cm
(11 inches)

KEY to Section
A off on switch
B control lamp
C starter switch for session
D Electronic counter or sequence
E Inlet and dimmer unit
EI Inlet and dimmer unit for G
EII Inlet and dimmer unit for H
F Working light
G Therapy light
H Complementary light

Fig 4.5

Therefore we can say that quality and quantity of light are recorded and accepted as a guide to adjust the body almost instantaneously at a speed which varies from not much slower than the speed of sound and up to almost the speed of light.

Thereby a human instrument receiving a colour will select the colour degree suitable for the individual person and his/her needs from the Colour Therapy Instrument.

Should the filter be very narrow, (See Fig. 4.1) – the thinner and peak line, peaking at about 18, there would only be one person receiving the correct colour of this filter. Since, however, such poor quality filters must not be used – our filters are valid for a thousand different patients who need that particular colour.

The Colour Therapy Instrument has these very beautiful healng filters. Since Quartz is the lesser brother of Diamond; these filters which we cut are the very best available today, obviously also expensive. But where human health is to be maintained or regained, only the best is just about good enough.

Brief description of use and reasons for the Colour Therapy Instrument

Hygeia Studios have been involved in the use of colour since 1956 and base their work on the findings and previous research of J. W. Von Goethel 1756–1832, and Rudolf Steiner 1861–1925. We have also taken into consideration more recent research and are Founder members of the Light and Health Research Council (M.L.H.R.C.)

Illumination: is available through natural light and this always remains the most beneficial light for the health of people. The harnessing of illumination through electricity, based on the incandescent Tungsten filament, as was discovered by Eddison, is still the best artificial illumination, albeit, not perfect.

The Thermal inertia of the normal Tungsten filament light produces a very gentle wave pattern as metal used for the glowing element will never go out once switched on. This stands in sharp contrast to fluorescent light which has up to now most frequently still an on and off cycle of 50 cycles positive to 50 cycles negative. Our Colour Therapy Instrument is supplied with special day-light equivalent tungsten bulbs.

Rhythm: We have developed out of the knowledge that rhythms are important aspects for human health, the rhythms used for the Colour Therapy Instrument. The rhythms which we use are developed from the Golden Mean phenomena which has a surprise element built into its structure and yet remains in harmony with the human being as a whole.

Form: We have also found that light changes its quality and structure depending on the aperture (windows) through which it is projected. This leads us to link colour to form. Through many years of research we have come to develop the forms most harmonious to the eight colours which are used for the Colour Therapy Instrument. We are, in this way, in COLOUR RHYTHM and FORM, able to offer this Colour Therapy Instrument for use in Clinics and places where complementary healing is conducted.

The Filters: The glass which is used for the seventeen filters is craftsman made and carries the vibrations of the glass blower's breath. Also we ensure that the glass which we put into filters is always stained by the three important metals – Gold (red), Silver (blue), Copper (all other colours, as copper oxide is capable of producing a very great range of colours. It is also known as the healing metal for many ailments).

Assessment: Those people who are sensitive, and there is an increasing number of these, will know how important it is to offer Colour Therapy in its many different forms. We find that coloured light is capable of controlling an incredible amount of molecular structure changes, such as blood pressure, cancer, migraine, and asthma, to mention just a very few of the problems which respond most adequately to colour. Diagnosis for colour therapy at Hygeia is made through the ancient art of dousing which has proven to be a most accurate tool, although other methods may be equally valid.

Practical: Upon the sale of our Colour Therapy Instrument we are prepared to give a day's instruction, and answer all questions which the buyer may like to put to us, and in the radius of one hundred miles the transport and travelling expenses are included in the price. Longer distances will by necessity have to be compensated, and a day's instruction carries a fee. *(See Price List and Introduction Charges.)*

Colour in Education

It has become quite evident that in most educational systems the subject of colour is vastly underrated as to its importance to all people in all walks of life. Since 1967, Theo Gimbel has spoken and published, and has been reported in the media worldwide on the knowledge of colour, yet its use is only known to a very few specialists and even in these circles the knowledge seems to be so narrow that most of these who know something about it, far from having a general foundation in all of its powerful aspects, know only a very limited amount related directly to their work.

In the work which Theo Gimbel has undertaken some surprising facts have come to light which touch many important areas of our daily life. Research increasingly shows the importance of light upon the harmonious functioning of the human body. Qualified light, i.e. coloured light, can be harnessed to produce specific effects. Colour can not only change moods as is now frequently reported in a great number of magazines, but causes even physiological changes, that can be measured, which affect wellbeing or indeed its opposite. All biochemical structures are influenced by colour; decoration is only a beginning. What is far more powerful is the use of colour in illumination. There it seems the comparatively small changes can have very big results in beneficial or detrimental influences on the environment. In people's working spaces illumination can be responsible for the smooth and error free running of an office, but can, conversely, make it a very tense and stressful area.

Colours can change the whole atmosphere of a place, especially when it is conveyed by light. The science behind it is hardly understood, let alone put into practice.

Hygeia Studios is a research centre, founded by Theo Gimbel, looking for support that, at least in this country, a serious start be made to bring this subject into the general curriculum of schools. The kind of support we need is for people to come forward and give their help in the following ways:

(1) Get in touch with us and be prepared to speak on this issue to as many people as they can.

(2) To promote colour as a subject in their schools, where we can offer constructive advice on how to approach this field.

Form, Sound, Colour and Healing

(3) Offer us opportunities to speak at board meetings, societies, gatherings of industry and commerce and educational bodies.

(4) Last, but not least, to provide funds to enable this work to continue and be made more widely known.

We have a group of people who are well-trained and can be contacted for this purpose.

Theo Gimbel hopes that there will be fellow humans who feel like he does, that this is a valuable subject to be taught in schools and indeed in all places of learning.

Eye Strength

Too often in modern life our eyes are forced to retain the same focusing distance. Driving, watching TV, reading for too long, working with VDU screens; none of this is a very good exprience for our eyes.

Our Eye Strengthening Chart is effective because it re-enlivens the activity of one's eyes by the power of colour.

(a) Looking at the blue and then at the red makes the eyes focus in totally different ways – the iris is revitalised.

(b) Colour perception depends on the arrangements that the rods and cones take up.

Each change of colour produces a new pattern. So, here again, strong concentration on each colour of the Eye Chart in turn takes the order of this fine colour-sensitive tissue into extremes of its capacity, thereby giving exercise to the eye as a whole.

Do your exercise regularly with this chart and you will reap real benefits!

BLUE   RED

Fig 4.6 see colour page (xiv)

Develop from indications given by J. W. von Goethe (1810) and Rudolf Steiner, (1919–1924).

Hygeia Studios have researched into this valuable way to help keep mobile the human eye and can now offer this chart as a useful tool for many people. The card can be stood up at eye level and used under good day-light conditions, (near a window in bad weather or winter).*

Let your eyes rest on the blue and 'soak in' this colour until a luminous area appears around the octagon shape and the colour of the shape itself begins to change. Then look at the white middle until a luminous, now glowing light appears. Let this fade and then rest your eyes on the red octagon again for a while until the same glow and change of colour appears around the red.

Return to the white centre and now see the whole glow appear again. Look for as long as it takes for this to gradually fade out.

Then return to the blue and repeat this for four to seven times, finishing up with the blue, not the red.

Do this daily, once or twice.

This will offer your eyes valuable help, and often returns lost energy. You will see that the colours call up each their own complementary hue.

Thoughts on our Communication with Self and others

Healing is not only repairing all things to be in their perfect state, it is also to balance, or regenerate, life in the patient who seeks the therapist, doctor, the healer, or even the best friend. But the patient has to be ready to understand and to accept, but most of all, to truly wish to return to a state, or rather to enter the new state of health, i.e. rebuilding of tissue which has been taken away through operations and in all cases harmonise the body.

Colour can open up in such cases the mind and harmonising thoughts which are the first steps to carry into the body new

*Hygeia Publications, 1976. Brook House, Avening, Tetbury GL8 8NS.

energies and accept a creative peace. From there it will sink into the emotional being and harmonise the inner experiences in the soul of a patient. This will, in turn, effect the metabolic etheric energies and bring life, flow, movement into the chemistry of the body tissue. When such gradual and patient development is brought into a real understanding and is lovingly accepted, then the physical conditions are so much at peace that lastly the tensions of the physical, metabolic, emotional and mental bodies can let the deep sub-conscious, creative energies (sexuality) bring about a real building up of tissue which can repair and adjust the new conditions in very surprising ways.

It is, then that the super conscious, the self (spirit), touches the body and communicates with the reproductive system which is now used to maintain the tool which often uses the etheric energies to live here on earth. Then the cell memory can become the power of the divine image of God which rays through again.

This can only happen when the blocks between mind, emotion, and metabolism are removed and/or harmonised.

Then, only then, do the blocks become pillars of strength. Colour can by experiences loosen up and regenerate all these bodies, a bridge is built by human beings to make links which are there by natural events, but are broken so that higher consciousness can be achieved.

Fig 4.7

Yes, such views might sound callous or cruel when so much suffering is endured by so many. We are however now learning in science and in spiritual development to overcome pain. Much is due because a more well developed consciousness, (mind over matter?!) or deeper understanding is being achieved. All this is the effort to develop a godlike person to become co-creators and conductors of personal and universal destiny. Those who swim across leave nothing behind, it is like a mental picture of crossing over but it fades. Most when challenged to build a bridge find this impossible.

This creates the first 'block' where we do not believe that there is a bridge between the spirit and the physical world. So we meet our first obstacle or block most of us cannot link the two worlds either we are too much earth bound and everything must be explained in terms of science, we have solid blinkers so that we do not see any disturbing visions that could upset the applecart. Insecurity can be so material that no reliance is there except that of this world which can be weighed measured and counted.

Others of us stand aloof on the high mountain where the light is always beautiful, details in the valley are not to be seen, they could mean work or are often unworthy, dirty and do not belong in this world of beauty and aloofness.

. . . a spinster lady dressed so perfectly in pink and white silk used to walk into this school for mentally handicapped children, she came to bring beauty to those less fortunate children. She used to sit on the table, her legs on the seat of a chair, (so not to touch too much of this unworthy earth). The class of some twelve 13 year old children was learning the poem about the beautiful butterfly. After several lessons conducted by this lady sitting perched 'on high' she said one day in a delicate high voice "Now my dear children we have said this beautiful poem about our butterfly often enough surely Johnny you can come forward and say it to the class". Johnny moved forward his eyes fixed upon the seated lady, he faced her, stooped a little and looked up and in his rather low earthly voice said "Pink knickers and suspenders!" The lady did not believe her ears, she staggered down from her high perch and fled the classroom in tears exclaiming – "these dirty unworthy children have no sense for beauty, I will not come again." Johnny was unaware of the earthing effect he had on the lady. Such characteristics are at this point blocks and should be understood, such persons need as much help as those with blinkers which prevent any spiritual images.

So we have to take first a little boat which is guided along a rope and then we will make a more tangible link but not too permanent as yet, take a client, from either side, across and see how much the images can become more feasible. First in their minds, after a while a link of inner experience through the strength of the image. It can become even a compulsive picture, how can I get my horse and cart across? (this is the picture of the soul and the body).

In the following four cases it will be seen how two of the patients are at this state, as yet unsuccessful, and cannot get out of their non-communicating conditions and the other two are more successful.

Colour Therapy, diagnostic findings

It becomes quite clear that we can assess the progress patients make in accordance with the links which occur during a sequence of treatment.

We should look at the five possible steps which can be taken when we are in control of our body, which is the recording instrument of our various functions.

The way we use these and understand such 'contacts' can be of very significant importance. We can call this making a bridge between the invisible self and what first touches down into our slightly more tangible area, or Mentality–Ego–Thoughtfield.

The cosmic, spiritual world is received in our head and through this we make the images; are inspired with ideas. It is then that we have to link these ideas, (ideals) to the mental, the yellow realm with which we make the concepts about the earth. Next we must enter our emotional being and integrate what we have received in the mental realm into the Astral–Soul entity of ours, here seen in blue. This has further to be transferred to our metabolic existence, the earthly etheric self in green. From there we also need to make the real link with the manifested world, the

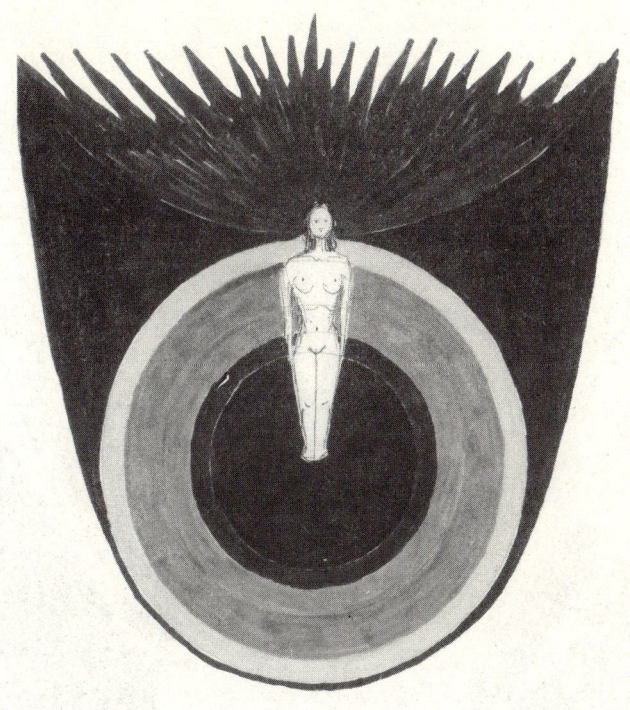

Fig. 4.8 see colour page (xv)

physical subconscious–sexual existence, here shown in red, the strong earth colour which also ensures our physical self to continue on this planet.

The magenta colour has been used to illustrate the cosmic-spiritual world which enters our heads.

The human form which finally incarnates into the physical body from the pure spirit form, the mental Ego, the emotional Astral or Soul to the physical–etheric. The only visible part is the form of the body itself.

Many people are not aware of the meaning of thoughts. These can come and go and nothing, or very little, is done about such communications. We do not seem to know where these originate, or do we?

More and more people begin to wake up to the questions: who are we, what is our purpose? Answers are not found unless there is a conversation. Conversations take place between two forces,

Form, Sound, Colour and Healing

See colour page (xvi)

people or energies. So we now make our first link between spiritual, self superconsciouness and mental, ego, thoughts.

In order to arrive at a harmonious whole, this first link must become inspired to make the next communication. Much gets stuck here as we have been taught to face our lives with the 'stiff upper lip' – but if we allow that the mental area is now to come into contact with the emotional, we can be moved to express what is given to us in the first link; we can express joy, sorrow, peace or restlessness. In this expressing, our mental experiences, we induce into our system a chemical change. This may be very fine and work very gently only, or it can become strong and cause what other people call a nervous breakdown. Such a happening is a drastic chemical change and it can loosen old stuck-fast experiences which should not have been allowed to become static. Most of those who are carefully guided through this big change become very sensitive people who are fit for very fine help on the level of psychic and spiritual work.

The changes which are allowed to be made by the individual person must further communicate through to the metabolic level where the direction of the spiritual self has made the mental contact, then the emotional reaction to this contact now allows the etheric energies to become involved. However, the work is not done unless this metabolic reaction is furthermore brought into the physical body where the final healing can take place.

Thus we build bridges between the spirit–Self, superconscious (magenta), the mental–Ego–Thought (yellow), Emotional–Astral–soul, (blue), metabolic–etheric–life (green) and the physical–sexual–subconscious (red). Only when all the arches are made to get across the 'river' can full health become a reality. In the following cases we can see the efforts made to the aspects in practical, day to day reactions, to Colour Therapy. If bridges are not made, eventually then the purpose of life is not fulfilled. If bridges are not made immediately then the efforts, made at the time, are stored up until the 'patient' is ready to make these, so in a way nothing is lost. We take four cases here and examine the outcome over seven sessions, during which a patient has responded, or not responded, to colour therapy.

It would, at this time, not yet be possible to be in absolute rhythmic control over our selves, but in the course of days, weeks and months we can say that all incarnated people build the necessary bridges between the realms mentioned above.

The pathological, or state of illness, occurs when one or the other bridge is too rarely made, or in severe cases not made at all, for some long time. Colour Therapy in conjunction with counselling can help to establish such links but we must allow

Form, Sound, Colour and Healing

the client (patient) to do this out of his/her own volition. We can only offer the insight into this to the patient, in other words, be the cosmic representative and inspire, give ideas, ideals, to the person which can reach into his/her as yet unrecognised inspiration. Making images to build bridges eventually must be undertaken by each person independently.

Let us examine what we can 'read' from these four examples.

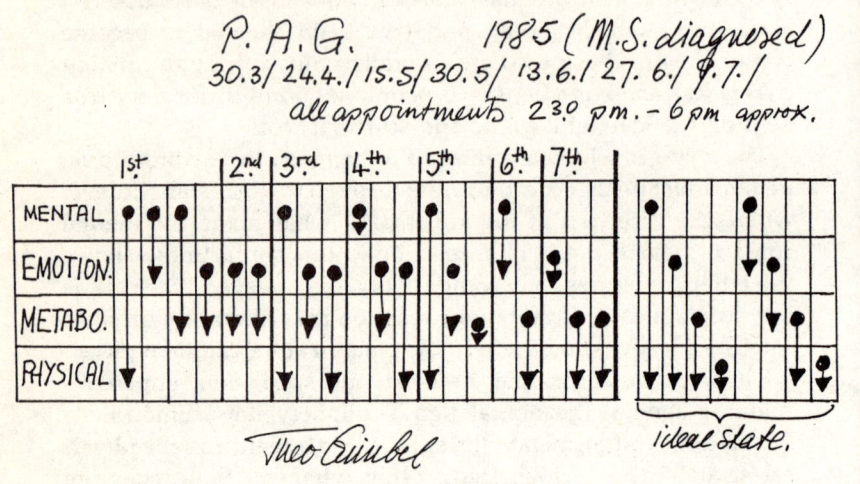

P. A. G.   1985 (M.S. diagnosed)
30.3/ 24.4./ 15.5/ 30.5/ 13.6./ 27.6./ 9.7./
all appointments 2.30 pm. – 6 pm approx.

Fig 4.9

First case

1st Tr. Mental attempts to communicate to physical, emotional and metabolic.

Emotional to metabolic very hopeful. Great anticipation mainly stemming from the mental (yellow area) to get better. This effecting the emotional (blue area). Lower emotional entering with the metabolic system. No direct links between metabolic and physical area (red). Only a mental to physical link which remains at this point a dream which can not yet be realised.

2nd Tr. Two efforts are made from the emotional to the metabolic. P. was impatient and restless, he could not control his behaviour.

3rd Tr. One attempt is made from the mental to the physical, one from the emotional to the metabolic, that last (3rd), from the emotional to the physical.

4th Tr. P. is remaining in his mental being unmovable; emotional to metabolic area is operating and the emotional to physical link is made. The challenges which we have carefully proposed are only considered at present. His nurse is prepared to help but for anyone to be cured the will to be well must come from within the communications made by the patient. P. is at present not prepared to put anything into the physical world; there are six blocks already which indicate that the 'messages' between the metabolic area and the physical do not function.

5th Tr. Mental to physical. Yes P. is thinking about it. He makes one attempt from the emotional to the metabolic and metabolic activity is happening.

6th Tr. No links between the emotional and the metabolic, but one first attempt between the metabolic and physical. The separation between the emotional and metabolic is shown. P. avoids to harmonise his whole person.

7th Tr. Stuck in the emotional realm and making two bridges: metabolic to physical. The communication patterns remain broken throughout the whole treatment.

Summing up
There are 7 attempts in the mental area to cope with the condition.
  9 Emotional attempts
  4 Metabolic
  3 Mental reach into the Physical
  2 Mental are stuck in the Emotions

The 9 emotional efforts get stuck in the metabolic system where there are only 3 links, (last three treatments made to mobilise the physical). However the mental efforts are absent and no one treatment shows what we are aiming at i.e. total body–metabolic–emotional – mental cooperation.

The aim is to teach the Patient through Colour Therapy to make all links happen. *See; 'ideal state'.*

When P. finally got the bridges built which could make him recover the links between the mental and metabolic (etheric) energies are failing him. Therefore we have only prepared a healing for later.

Later may not be in this lifetime; (no efforts of any help, be it whatever is ever wasted, it becomes a matter of time.)

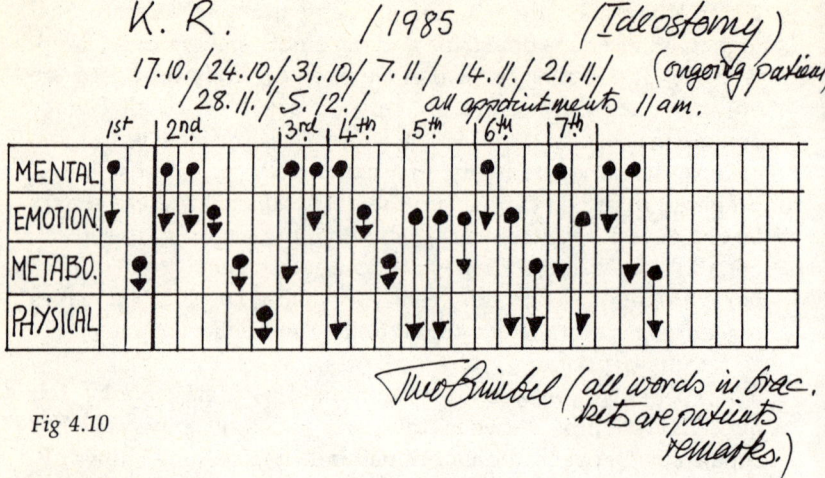

K. R.   /1985   (Ideostomy)
17.10./24.10./31.10./ 7.11./ 14.11./ 21.11./ (ongoing patient)
28.11./ 5.12./ all appointments 11am.

	1st	2nd	3rd	4th	5th	6th	7th
MENTAL							
EMOTION.							
METABO.							
PHYSICAL							

Fig 4.10

Theo Gimbel (all words in brackets are patients remarks.)

Second case

1st Tr. Very detached, touched by the experience of the colour therapy session. Aware of her metabolic system (I felt a great warmth and tingling in my hands)

2nd Tr. Two efforts are made from the mental into the emotional. Aware of emotions but not linked, aware of metabolic but not linked, aware in physical but no bridge made between the upper areas.

3rd Tr. Mental to Metabolic area, it is seen as progress. (Since I came to you I am for the first time in ten years out of pain) I remarked that she must now be careful not to do things which because of the warning pain, could upset her. Mental to emotional link made.

4th Tr. Mental to physical state link made. Inter communication within emotional and metabolic state, but as yet no links other than awareness.

5th Tr. This shows improvement as a mental to the emotional state is made and two bridges built to link the emotional to the physical. (There is family upset, her son has been very negative.) I advised to bear it in silence and think positive thoughts but not to try and contact him directly.

6th Tr. Treatment all but one bridge is made. Very good. Mental to emotional; emotional to physical and metabolic to physical the only one not made is emotional to metabolic. In K's state this is the most difficult one naturally.

Form, Sound, Colour and Healing

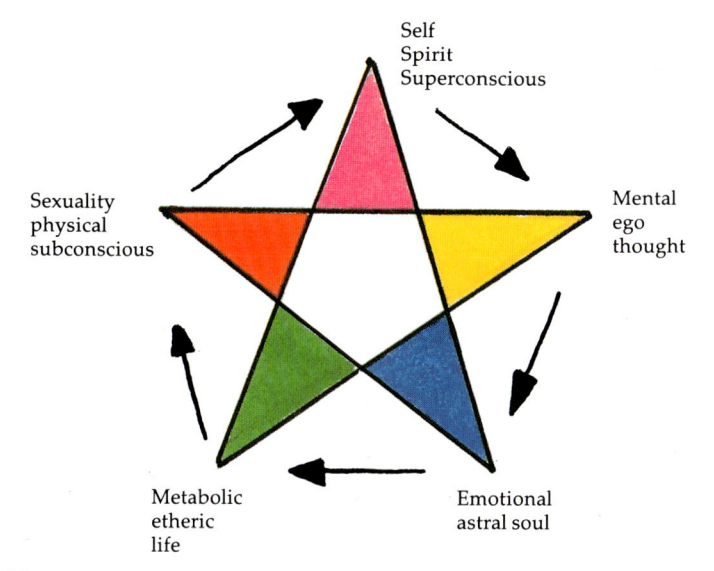

Fig 3.14 see page 95

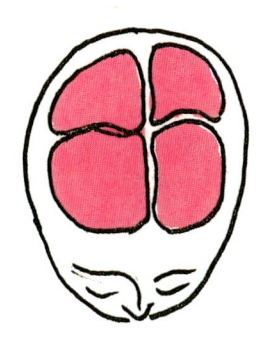

Fig 3.16 see page 103

(ix)

Form, Sound, Colour and Healing

Fig 3.15 see page 97

(x)

Form, Sound, Colour and Healing

Fig 3.17 see page 106

Form, Sound, Colour and Healing

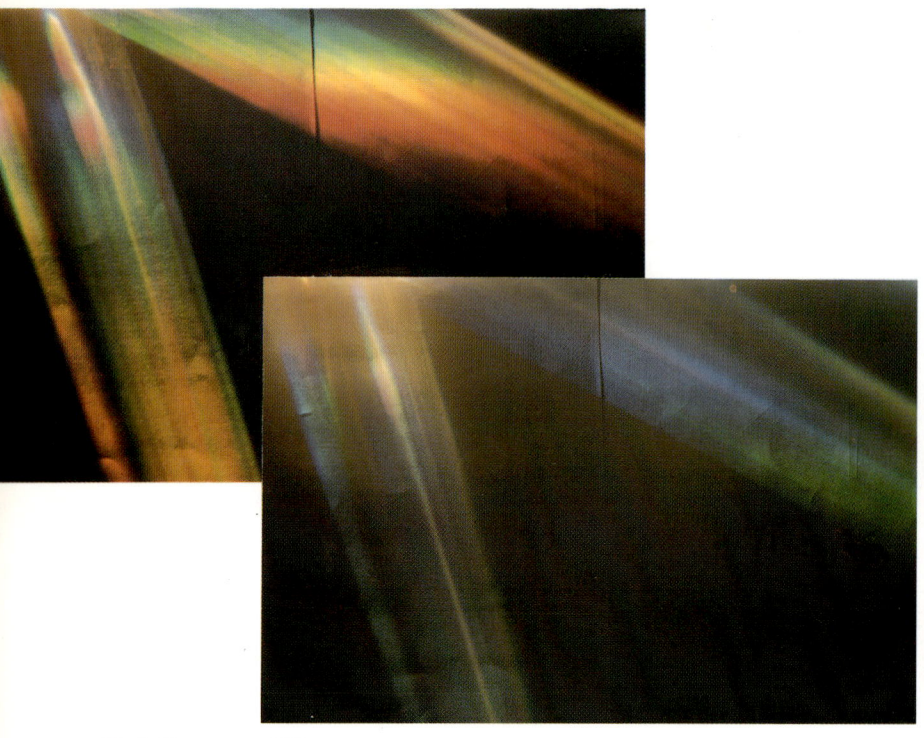

Fig 3.18 see page 107

Form, Sound, Colour and Healing

See page 111

Form, Sound, Colour and Healing

Fig 4.6 see page 118

(xiv)

Form, Sound, Colour and Healing

Fig 4.8 see page 123

Form, Sound, Colour and Healing

See colour page 124

7th Tr. Mental–Metabolic and emotional–Physical.
8th Tr. This is very good: a mental link is made to the emotional and metabolic and from there to the physical. Within a week K has made all bridges which is a very good sign. (Her neighbours are most interested in her better looks she is bearing a smile, her skin is much more alive and she seems to be more cheerful.)

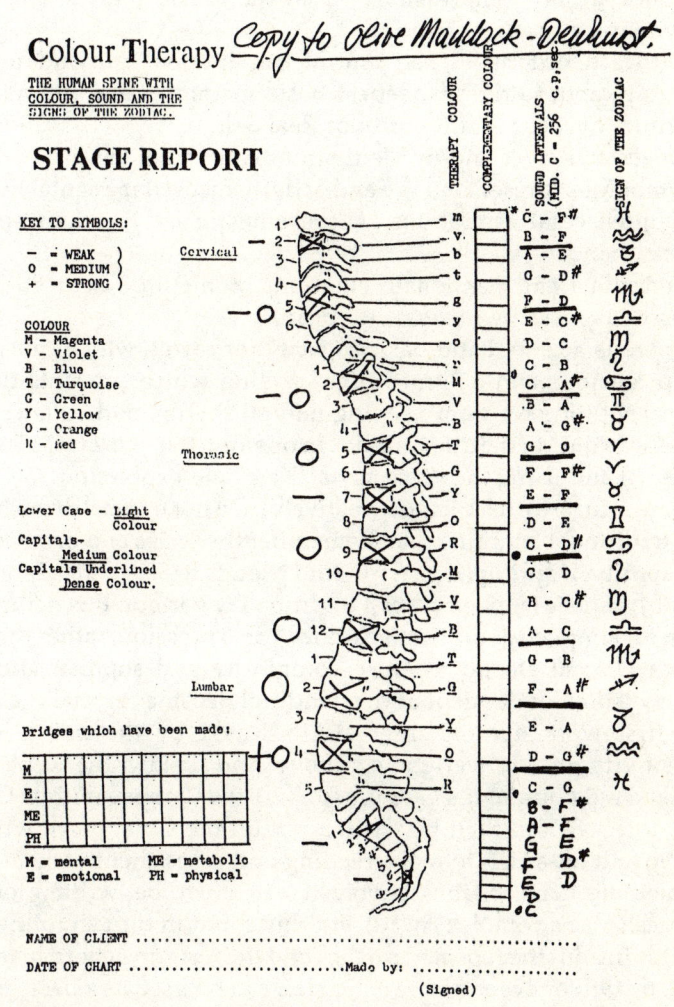

Fig 4.11

Olive Maddock-Dewhurst is our music Therapist also a qualified Colour Therapist (MIACT LRAM).

(All patients receive a music tape to accompany their colour therapy sessions, this is an example of music.)

K	R

These are my "impressions" from the music and the chart; they may be useful: I hope so!

Outward order and self-control but hidden fear and uncertainty about origins, deepest basic memories and ultimate Spiritual purpose and identity of Real Self.

Need for Prayer and/or Meditation. Ante-natal or very early trauma? Most present energy and activity focused in mental life, and intellectual aspirations. A great desire for Freedom and "Clean hands".

Tenacious and passionate emotions. Sometimes accused of "possessiveness by nearest and dearest".

There is a central and basic capacity for revolt, which causes deep tensions and a "knife-edge" feeling which prevents the physical processes from keeping natural rhythm and balance.

A "way out" of the dilemma lies in opening the *centre* (5th. Tur. Unison) and using the voice as its "Key" and expression. (5 Cr. Green. min. 3rd). (Use hands creatively). Do not feel restricted by the traditional feminine role. Remember the scales and balances of Eternity. If appropriate, try to find friends to *Sing with*. (Duets ideal!) – music (& poetry?) of a traditionally harmonious nature. Aim for simplicity and "transparency" of expression, rather than Great Drama! Do not confuse complexity and sophistication with wisdom or depth of understanding! Become "crystalline!".

I first work out the intervals indicated by the points of sensitivity of the vertebrae, above and below the central 'balancing' point of the G–C unison (viz the G above middle C). The intervals can then be written out on the Great Stave with treble and bass clef, to make reading and assessment early and immediate. The pitches involved can then be written out vertically, as a complex chord, and this chord in turn simplified by leaving out the repeated pitches and the resulting chord of the 17th or 19th or even greater extension can be used as a basis for harmonic exploration. The voice or voices can offer the ideal

Fig 4.12

instrument for extemporization, but the wide range of pitch makes this impracticable. Any instrument can be used, although the keyboard instrument provides the greatest possibilities for the solitary performer.

I follow a pattern of exploration in this sequence:

(a) The intervals at the pitch indicated by the Spine Chart.
(b) The complete 'chord'.
(c) From the lowest upward, the intervalular* qualities separately explored throughout the range of the instrument used.
(d) Melodic patterns derived from above.
(e) Rythmic variations.
(f) Free improvization based on the foregoing experience.

Throughout the process, the intuition and intellect are employed in as balanced a way as possible. The concentration involved can awaken an intuitive sensitivity to the patient and

*I think Intervalic is better!!!

Form, Sound, Colour and Healing

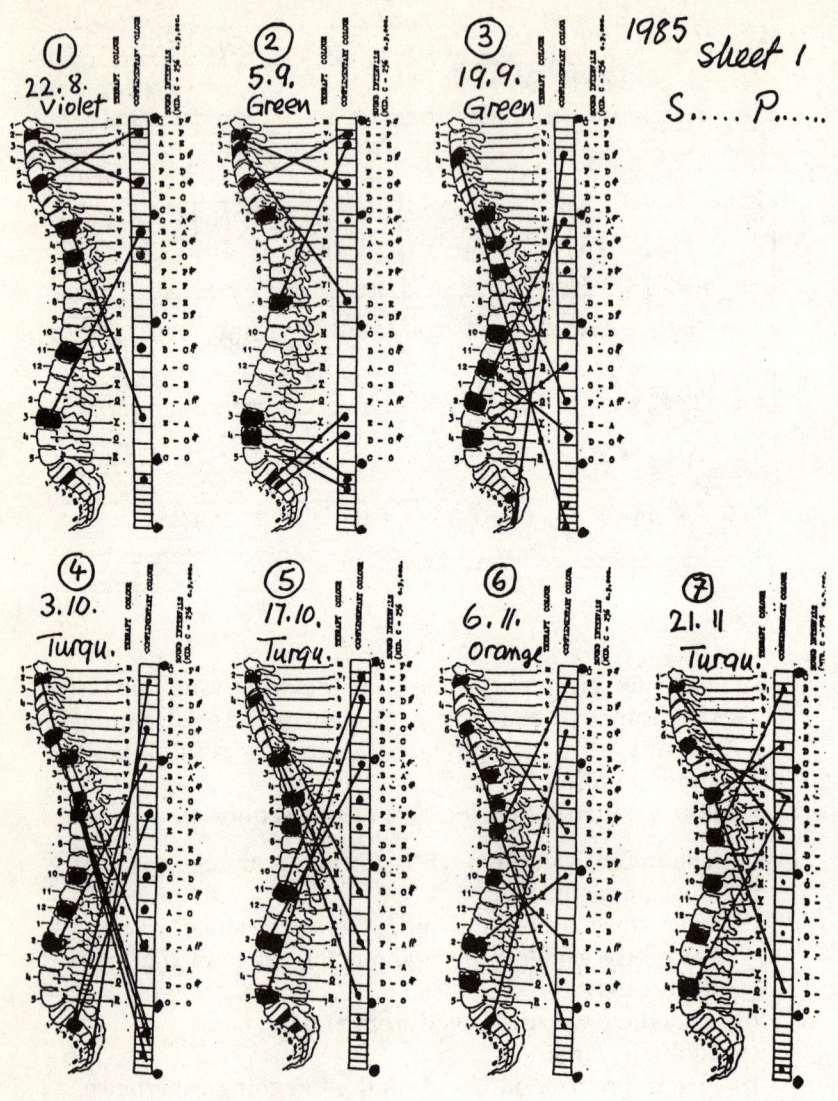

Fig 4.13

the impressions thus gained should be offered in a discreet and positive form – as being helpful ideas rather than "readings of destiny"!!!

Emphasis should be placed on the importance of silence – the matrix of music and upon the significance of Space in music, for the 'Sounds' are the points of a framework or lattice upon which the energy builds a resonant space – a crystal of music – perhaps the true meaning if the 'Crystal Spheres' we read about in poetry by mystical writers.

Olive Dewhurst-Maddock,
LRAM, ARCM,
Formerly Sadlers Wells Opera.

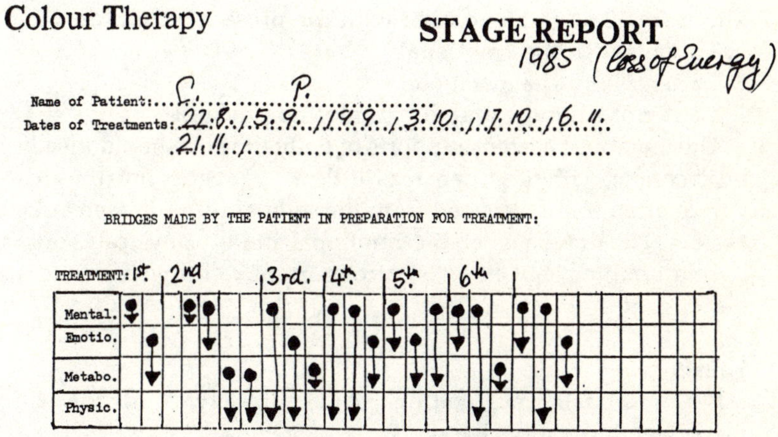
Colour Therapy
STAGE REPORT
1985 (Loss of Energy)
Name of Patient: S. P.
Dates of Treatments: 22.8./5.9./19.9./3.10./17.10./6.11./21.11./
BRIDGES MADE BY THE PATIENT IN PREPARATION FOR TREATMENT:
TREATMENT: 1st 2nd 3rd. 4th 5th 6th
Mental.
Emotio.
Metabo.
Physic.

Fig 4.14

Third case

1st Tr. Very slow to cooperate, however some temporary relaxing has been achieved.

2nd Tr. Somewhat better responses but no links between emotional and metabolic. This could account for her emotional exhaustion.

3rd Tr. Her responses are much increased. We do not get any lasting effects as yet.

4th Tr. To come to grips with her will (gut energy may be still very hard.) There is an over activity in her mentality.

5th Tr. Why is S.P. so tired and unable to cope she is not making any attempt to reach down into her body and all the efforts are stuck?

6th Tr. Looking back S.P. is frightened to make contact with her emotional self. Very few attempts are made to let this emotion reach into her metabolism which would react and promote the flow of energy.

7th Tr. It becomes very clear that S.P. will have to continue to come. It's also very obvious that she does not only avoid to communicate with her own body but also with other people.

Summing up

There are 12 attempts to cope with the present conditions
   5 attempts in the emotional
   4 attempts in the metabolic
   1 attempt from the emotional into the physical

The metabolic system supports of daily life and should ideally be in contact with the other areas, little thought goes into the area where attention is directed from the mental into the metabolic system. The link between the emotional and the physical is only once attempted, but not very strong to make things come to a better unity.

Fourth case

1st Tr. Mentally not letting go of old styles of life etc mental–emotional bridge.

Mental–physical, trying to link joy with peace in her work. Emotional – metabolic very weak link which results in her general condition which is not necessarily physical. We are working on this in counselling.

Metabolic to physical also weak, we are not able to work this out at present but it will be found so I said to H.L.

The physical link within this area indicates her will to cope but there are gaps which we must find. Red to stimulate.

2nd Tr. Attempts are made to communicate with her whole being but something is stuck, in the psychic. There is no way to rush this treatment. Orange to lighten depression.

3rd Tr. – incl 5th Tr. We seem to get only temporary help and yet there is an effort made all the time which is however not sustained we talked over each time why? Violet to restore self respect and dignity.

Colour Therapy — STAGE REPORT 1985

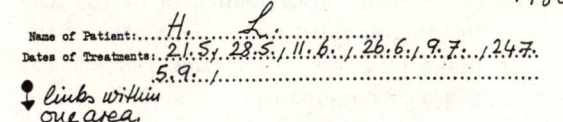

Name of Patient: H. L.
Dates of Treatments: 21.5./ 28.5./ 11.6./ 26.6./ 9.7./ 24.7./ 5.9./

↓ links within one area.

BRIDGES MADE BY THE PATIENT IN PREPARATION FOR TREATMENT:

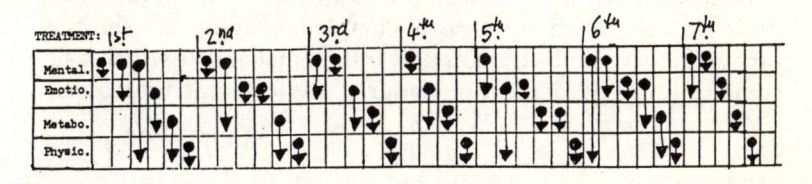

TREATMENT: 1st 2nd 3rd 4th 5th 6th 7th

TREATMENT COLOUR:

Fig 4.15

6th Tr. Suddenly we are making progress. This treatment has resulted in excellent progress. Her mother had never forgiven her for having had such a very special link with her father who had died two years ago.

We talked about letting hate become peace and love. All links are suddenly made and her energies are coming back. H.L. is making all the necessary links.

7th Tr. H.L. has really achieved with the Colour Therapy an re-enlivening of her person. She rests in a way effortless in each area just a slight movement from the mental into the emotional. Blue to create peace and calm within her, reduce any leftover tensions.

TREATMENT:

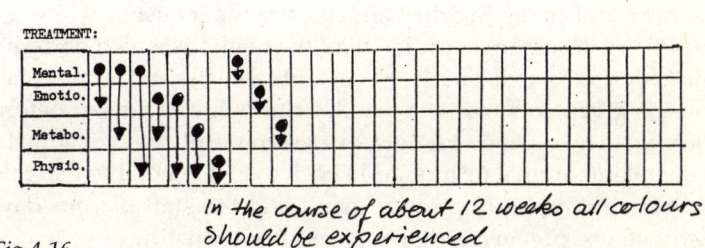

In the course of about 12 weeks all colours should be experienced

Fig 4.16

All seven communications are made and this pattern cannot be maintained by many, if at all by any person. What appears is that it is interdispersed over days, weeks, yes, over the lifetime. In young children more easily but in adults blocks appear which prevent the free flow between the four realms of being. The message is that we receive into our spirit–self superconscious the information and then make this into our mental images, the thoughts by way of our Ego or personality.

We can only strive to fully communicate and such human beings who have achieved such states are rare. It is the aim for all to do this by which we become complete conductors over our own self. There is no stronger power than that of love which will communicate without fear or favour, it just loves and thereby is.

The Patient turns into a Healer

It is a spiritual law, that if you have found a way to heal, or you have been led by a fellow human being to discover how to heal yourself you must teach others who are seeking you out for help. Of course you may refer them to a therapist you think can help also; but the first steps must be given by you who has found health.

Trust that you find the words which are the right ones at the time you are helping another human. Experience has always been that you will feel absolutely inadequate at the time, especially in the early stages, when you begin this acceptance of handing on. Inadvertently you are by this way discovering also more and more how to be yourself increasingly better. In no uncertain terms you are teaching through you as you are also taught. In a strange way you are out of time and space as both teaching and being taught happens simultaneously.

It is very necessary to understand the methods which underlie this new stage when a patient turns into a healer and so you may now be given this following dedication which you say before you start to help another fellow, even if you apply your healing to stone, plant, animal or human in each case it is good to use this dedication. You end up really using it at the start of your day, then you are preparing yourself for all eventualities.

A Dedication for a Healer
(Remember that you are the channel and not the energy itself, this will flow through you and is not of you.)

I ask to be free of myself,
I am protected by a more advanced being (or beings)
I am a channel for the power of wholeness
   (My concept of wholeness is in harmony through the communication, communion.)
My states of my personal needs are in the hands of this high being.
I am touched through and through to my subconscious
I am now prepared to do healing through me.

I am in the right place
   at the right time
   for the right purpose.   Amen

Chapter 5

A Threefold Approach to a Patient – Involved Therapy

As we move into the future it seems now indicated that more and more health must come from the direct involvement of the patient with his/her own illness. To study the problem and learn with the aid of the doctors and therapists to overcome the fear aspect and take an objective stand towards the affliction.

To know is to help and fear prevents the active participation of the patient to co-operate in his/her recovery.

An exciting new aspect of Therapy seems to open up for all human beings through the study of three dimensional space and the experience of colour together with the mathematical knowledge of the only five regular solids called the Platonic Solids. Although it was before Plato's days, by the scientist of antiquity, Pythagoras, that the discovery of these solids was made.

Science has almost moved into such detailed aspects, that

coherence to the whole and the origin of knowledge is so obscure that only a few can actually retrace the steps.

Therefore, we need to go to the origins time to time and reappraise our position. Each time we go 'back' we also see from a new level of consciousness the original plan and usually quite considerable steps can be made into the present standing and beyond for the development of future ideas and practical application of the 'new' findings for the present moment onwards.

It all starts with the crystallisation when in whatever form of density, out of the liquid a molecule crystallises into a more solid form of matter.

Too many recent and present scientists have found evidence that life secrets are concealed in the microscopic world of the atom and that in these invisible areas is life, or a substance which seems to be, what they call: unstable; but apparently can behave according to the actual thought pattern of human investigators.

Many have not spoken about it as they feel unable to make statements on such an uncertain basis.

With many a wonderful human soul who was a scientist in the life last lived in physical state, many most valuable discoveries have gone unspoken, unwritten and not communicated because of the lack of courage to pronounce something in terms of a non-scientific form or statement.

Those who have done so risk their place as fellows of a socially accepted group of scientists, professors, etc.

But there will soon be a time when we will be unable to have at our disposal the intricate research machinery and the economical support of these highly sophisticated laboratories. And then: will all go under or will most of us awake to a moment when we, in the emergency of such conditions, find ways which may not be logical, but will prove to work?

Here we come to the point that has already been demonstrated over and over again that thought, light, colour plus sound can influence the actual final materialisation, or crystallisation of such matter which can take up form that may become plant, animal, mineral or as human beings. It is even now feasible that by the use of meditation of a carefully guided type alterations can be made on general and specific health patterns.

It seems that certain sounds can so change the cell structure of people that resistance to ill health is weakened even to the point that destruction of the form takes place. This may start in the loss of concepts of rhythms which are pulsating with the nature of our planet and thereby come into disorientation with time and space.

A Therapy which is of an upbuilding and re-establishing-of-health nature must be in harmony with the environment and with the human being who is able to change the rhythms and patterns.

Not only must we therefore reconsider the rhythms, but also the form or space element wherein the pulse is beating according to its particular form.

Salt crystal interlocking cubes

Let us state once more that there is no two-dimensional physical state, but that all is three dimensional. If we start with such a concept we open up fields which can be used therapeutically, a therapy that will start in our thought (thinking), sink into a relationship with self, or are felt (feeling) as Steiner uses the next lower realm and finally can become action (will).

Now we must start the study of the forms which can be 'created'; many will be arising out of certain frequencies of sound.

Hans Jenny in his research into Cymatics develops the most

A Threefold Approach to a Patient – Involved Therapy

exciting science out of which music therapy could find a new way of application. Experts who do know have stated that certain composers actually have some knowledge of the vibrations which their music produced and these can be translated into the crystallisation forms of certain Elements, such as salt (cubic), sulphur and mercury. Arpad Joo the conductor of the Calgary Symphony Orchestra, Canada, has researched into the compositions of J. S. Bach, where he finds not only complete mathematical harmony but also that an alliance with the chemical world. Steiner speaks of an energy which he calls "sound or chemical ether". This is very significant as it points to the direction in which we must move.

Salt has a certain form the image of which could be used to strengthen the body. It is in its structure, what is called a face centred cubic chemical when it crystallises into physical matter in music this is the area of rhythm and its rhythmic repetition of form in the Golden Mean relationship.

Its colour is deep green the colour of balance and partaking of the physical. Hexahedron.

Sulphur. This chemical has always been associated with the soul of man and in recent scientific research some of this link is found as psychology and physiology compare notes. In the structure it is classified as mono clinic rombohedral. The musical

Sulphur crystal orthorhombic

relationship is that of harmony. The harmony of the soul. The human soul has also a relationship with air and thus is related to the octahedron. ("The Five Platonic Solids," Hygeia Publication). Air in the old tradition is the gold-yellow colour because it has the power to exchange the energies very easily. This is why a completely yellow man-made environment is seldom beneficial.

The spirit of man is related to the element of mercury. This is a liquid crystal which shatters into a thousand little balls if dropped on a hard surface. Each of these being immediately again a sphere. The spirit is also the conducting energy of all those conscious clear thoughts of man. The musical connotations are the melody. Thus we have now to see it as the fire, the flame of God, its colour is red and the form is the Tetrahedral energy.

We can state that within the structure of any biological manifestation there seems a 'liquid' state that sooner or later can respond to environmental sounds. So there is a call for experts who will advise on music that can heal and thereby should be used more widely, or conversely give guidance as to what we should not use in sound as it can undermine our health body.[1]

It is the concern of all humans to learn today why and how life as we know it in the physical state is possible.

And like children in play find out, we do so in being interested emotionally, and actively involving ourselves with colour, sound and form.

In a practical study of diabetics we find the structure of insulin: *we here in our research at Hygeia are convinced that such a structure could be 'made' in the human body at the command of the correct visualisation of its structure. The concern of any patient with the cubic form, both mathematically, geometrically and artistically could restimulate the individual's cell structure to mobilise that activity consciously which in its subconscious natural state within the body has ceased to be produced or operating normally.

---

[1] The study of the five platonic solids is an important start, *Healing Through Colour*, Theo Gimbel, C. W. Daniel, 1980, sees the practical making and enjoying of these solids is a first step. "The Five Platonic Solids" ready to cut out of cardboard with instructions on how to make into a beautiful mobile *and* reference to their colour, elements and mathematical relationships are also available from us.

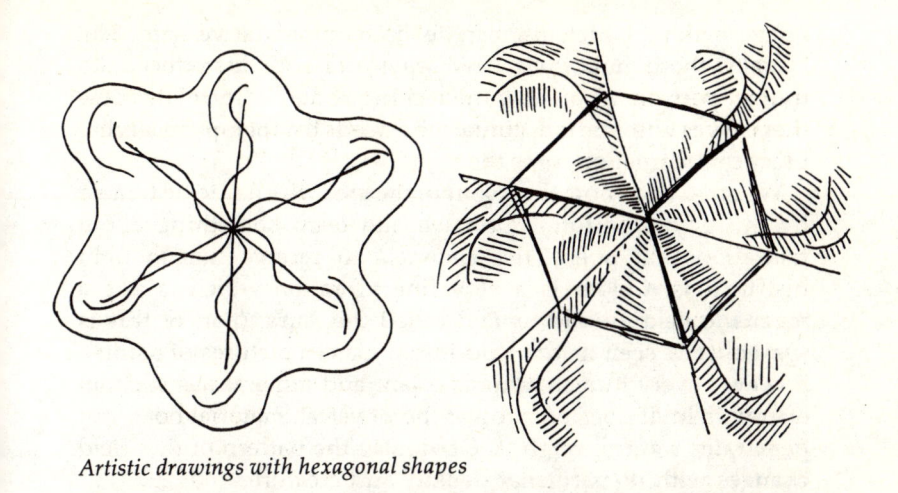

A Threefold Approach to a Patient – Involved Therapy

Artistic drawings with hexagonal shapes

We are taking here an example to show how we suggest the use of our research findings in a practical way.

It is suggested, from our recent research that: provided the individual does, in a meaningful rhythmic timetable during any week, make a conscious effort to work with the molecular structure which is at present missing in the body, there will appear a thought-programming of the mobile structure to reproduce the lacking energy.

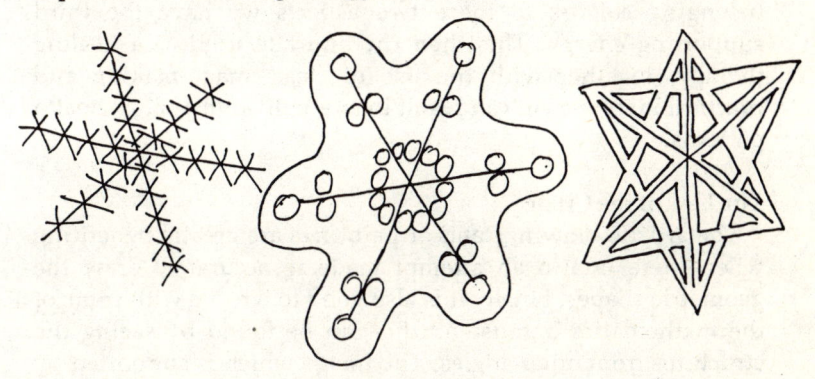

The patient can be lead to draw or paint the above and following patterns, which help the physical deficiency.

Thus we could look at such a therapy to provide a meaningful image-making which also can be called a meditative approach. Usually these important new ways must be introduced by trained persons who know the technique and who will involve themselves with the individual who needs the therapy by giving practical instruction.

We must also know the colour of the area which is to be treated by this rhythmic form approach and learn something about relaxation that opens the channels to receive our thought instructions. Colour is a very fine vibration which is like a magnetic field around us and called the Aura, (part of this is symbolically seen as the halo in old master pictures of saints), however every human, animal, plant and mineral has such an energy field. It does not stop at the physical, material body but penetrates right through it. Obviously the pattern of this field changes with its particular density and creature.

In the perfect being, especially if it is human laws of the colour spectrum apply, but we must admit that there is no perfect being incarnated in this physical world. By this fact we can actually strive to form the concept of perfection and call this aspiring to God.

The aspects of colour are well known in optics and scientifically clearly stated. (See *Healing Through Colour*.)

In this manner we will then find a co-operation between actual forms, the sounds and colours which support them and with the belonging colours to these two aspects we have the third supporting energy. This then rhythmically used as a healing therapy, together with the use of clear image-making and practical involvement can result in a re-enlivening of lost health patterns.

The Law of the Circle

The artistic drawings and or paintings are greatly benefiting when there is also an attempt made to accurately draw the geometric shapes. Finally it is also good to wrestle with some of the mathematics because all this can be found by seeing the structures from other angles. The image which is supported by many aspects is more vital and effective through the very effort in the search for the correct concept.

It is useful to concern oneself in the morning with the mathematical, in the midday with the geometrical and in the

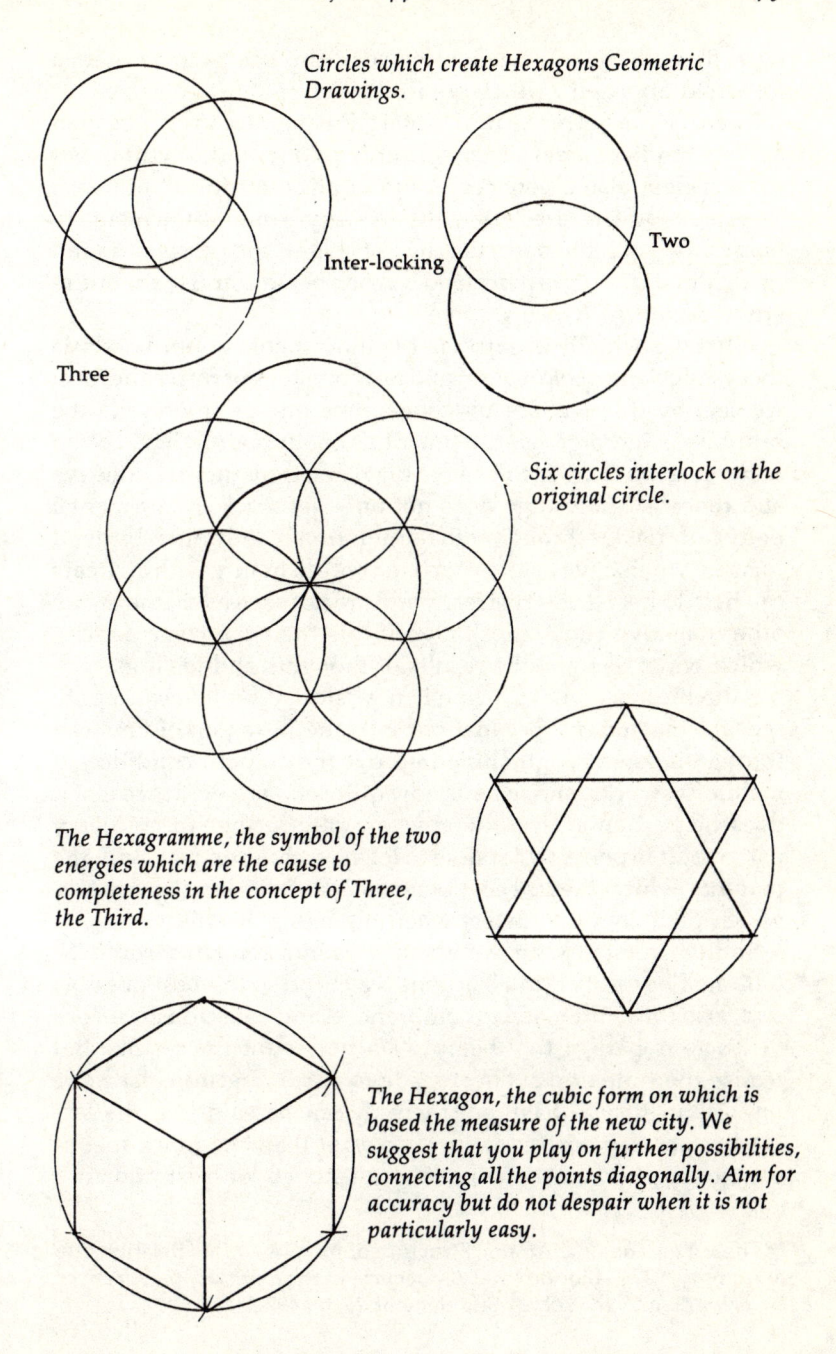

A Threefold Approach to a Patient – Involved Therapy

Circles which create Hexagons Geometric Drawings.

Three

Inter-locking

Two

Six circles interlock on the original circle.

The Hexagramme, the symbol of the two energies which are the cause to completeness in the concept of Three, the Third.

The Hexagon, the cubic form on which is based the measure of the new city. We suggest that you play on further possibilities, connecting all the points diagonally. Aim for accuracy but do not despair when it is not particularly easy.

evening with the artistic therapy work, this seems to be again a threefold approach, which we find so often most valuable.

There is a very precise individual adjustment to each person in all the applied areas, form, sound, colour and rhythm, but nevertheless also a generally valid application for all humans. The adaptations are made by a very fine attunement to harmonise with the particular hue of colour, the personal sound quality and the forms perceived by each person, and to the entire environment in which we live.

What we actually absorb via the movements of our hands as these touch and explore form and how our eyes perceive the form we see, by this we already programme our brain and via the pituitary gland organise the functions of our body. All that often remains to be done is to believe that such thoughts are effective and that the knowledge does not only get stuck in our mental body but trickles through into the emotional body often by good images which have even a touch of sentimentality within; (tears can help to heal if used correctly and are not seen as shame or any other negative experience). Out of this then can come activity which will make real the results of thoughts and feelings.

A preliminary pilot scheme is now started on this concept to see if a meaningful occupation with the hexagonal forms can through image strengthening improve the diabetic condition. If mediation works, and there is now quite enough evidence that it does help, then such a therapy can only further the recovery patterns. It is perfectly feasible to let even children play with the patterns which they need to enhance their lacking structures, which pathology can detect when there is a disability.*

So involvement with this therapy cannot remain theoretical, but must be applied in all artistic ways and to the best possible end, also the *effort* made to comprehend and consciously absorb the facts is part of the therapy. Do not count the results, but realise the time of real effort made to reach a result is far more important than to have got there. It can be said that the less intellectual approach is more successful than the quick intelligent grasp. And most of all banish all anxiety or frustration if it

---

* "Three-Dimensional Atomic Structure of Insulin and its Relationship to Activity," T. L. Blundell and Associates, in the *Journal of the American Diabetes Assoc. Inc.* Vol. 21 Supplement 2, pp. 492–505

seems difficult, offer what is not at this moment clearly understood to a loving state and say: "Well, I will know when its right to know." Also always offer gratitude for any step that is made.

We are not under pressure, but we should enjoy what we do. There is peace, time, space and relaxation. These concepts are almost missing now in our society. The mad rush, the competitive world has brought illness and unhappiness, so let there be peace, and health will ensue.

What is Colour? How does it appear in the material world that we see?

Colour as such, does not exist. It can be best defined as the ability of our eyes and our brains to distinguish between different wavelengths of light. Quite simply, different types of molecules absorb different wave bands of visible light, also different quantities of light, whilst giving off again the remaining parts of the spectrum. They are traditionally obtained from plants and from mineral oxides, but chemical research has added an enormous number of synthetic paints and dyes, vastly increasing the range of colours available to everyone, not only the rich.

Extremely fine, almost elusive quantities of these substances can alter the tones, hues, and shades of colour. These tones are also extremely sensitive to the kind of illumination under which they appear – not surprising, when we consider that man-made lights rarely match the spectrum of natural daylight.

Can Colour have any Measurable Effects, and if so, What?

Biological structures, plant, animal or human react to colour, whether this is an illumination or pigment. Illumination has an almost instantaneous effect; pigment is less pronounced.

The experiments which we have carried out are very simple but show absolutely repeatable results which anyone can reconstruct and prove for himself. Biological structures of plants are strongly influenced by the use of colour. *See *Growing Plants Under Colour*, Hygeia Publications, Theo Gimbel, 1973.

Generally, light is picked up by what we call eyes, but plants pick up light via their foliage. Coloured walls, curtains, small or large surfaces all produce changes in the cells of the eyes, and in all cells which are exposed to coloured pigments. A sensory organism must therefore be not only in those cells which choose to specialise and become actual eyes but in all cells, regardless of their location in the physical structures of plants, animals, and humans. ALL CELLS ARE LIGHT SENSITIVE, and a blind person is often more aware of colour than those of us with normal sight.

What is the Difference Between Coloured Pigment and Coloured Light?

Coloured walls, curtains, clothes, and any other pigment-coloured surfaces are only reflecting a colour, giving off the wavelengths of the spectrum that they cannot absorb. These colours are primarily experienced by the eye, and remind the observer of the colour which these objects display. Coloured pigments can alter the spatial perception of an object through their effect on the optical processes of the eye. For instance, if the same size rooms are painted, one in red; one in blue, then red will make the room appear smaller than it was; blue will make it appear larger than before.

Pigments also produce 'after-image' reactions in the eye. Look intently at any coloured surface for about fifteen seconds, then look away at a white surface and the complementary colour seems to appear there for a few seconds.

Under coloured illumination however, all pigment colours are changed. The space that is being illuminated becomes saturated with this colour and it is not possible to tell what the illuminating colour is without actually seeing the source, the lamp, itself.

Pigment colours are changed and altered in a manner which is not always predictable, as the hues which appear, display most delicate responses according to the very fine differences of texture and tone; this becomes very emphasized in textiles.

What is the Importance of Colour in our Daily Life?

The importance of colour is only just beginning to be considered,

A Threefold Approach to a Patient – Involved Therapy

and broadly speaking, most people are as yet unaware of the real powers which colours have in their use. By and large it is thought of as an aesthetic question which remains superficial, whereas the depth to which this colour question can be taken is really very profound indeed.

We shall look at the use of colour in our environment, in clothes, decor, illumination, and see what meaningful use can be made of it. There are several approaches:

(a) Psychological – Most importantly here, colours REMIND us of previous encounters with them, and associations based on earlier experiences. Whether we like a colour or not is often deeply linked in our minds to our first conscious experience of it, to the impression that the associated person or place made on us. It can also be that the effects of a colour build up gradually throughout our lives. For instance blue is usually considered as a 'cold' colour. In these latitudes it is often associated with the chill blue-white of snow, but suppose we considered it from the viewpoint of a dweller around the Mediterranean? Maybe it would still be 'cooling' but in how much more pleasant a way!

Red is another colour with strong associations – red is for fire, for warmth, but also means danger.

The colours that a person chooses to wear, or to have in their surroundings, can speak a great deal about their inner feeling states – as long as these colours have been freely chosen, without the pressure of what is 'fashionable.'

The conscious putting together of certain colours, or the taking of one colour and the toning it with various carefully planned shades, has infinite possibilities which may be 'pleasing' – 'chique' – 'beautiful' etc., but this 'fashionable' use always has an impact on another level, and does not remain at the psychological level where it started. This level is the:

(b) Physical – As a result of years of research which Theo Gimbel began in Bristol in 1956, it is not possible to think that we can use colour in any way whatsoever without involving the whole, and we mean the whole, of the plant, animal or human being. See *Healing Through Colour*, Theo Gimbel – C. W. Daniel Co Ltd. 1980.

It is well known that we can control human blood pressure, raising it through exposure to red light, or by wearing red clothes. Blue illumination or clothes have the opposite effect, the lowering of blood pressure. I am convinced that wild animals can be calmed by the use of deep blue light. (Research still remains to be done on this).

Clothes are colour filters, and we sin a great deal by our ignorance with regard to colours. Different colours worn over each other, behave like coloured mixtures, and can greatly influence the moods of people. The effect of colours in clothes is slower than the effect coloured illumination has on us; slower to arise, but also slower to subside. More women than men are colour conscious, and we believe this is a matter of tissue density (this is not yet proven, but is very plausible from the results of other research.)

Red and blue colours are known to markedly influence biological structures; all other shades of colour also have qualities which produce their own specific reactions. These may be either positive or negative, according to how colour is applied.

(c) Health – As colour, especially as illumination, has been shown to have marked effects on all living cells exposed to it, it follows that we can use these responses when necessary, to create healthier conditions within these cells. All cells in the human body are light-sensitive but also transparent to a greater or lesser degree, the skin especially so. Light can penetrate deep into the organs of the body, certain colours always having the same effects, regardless of where the cells are.

(d) Environmental – It can now be clearly seen that we could create environments for commerce, industry, hospitals, etc., which could give a one-sided advantage to a particular group of people, whilst another group is being 'exploited'. Colour is indeed manipulative, so let us be aware of its effects so that we can create an environment that is good for all, and realise that this knowledge is not a commodity to be 'sold' – a little here, and a little there – so that no one gets the 'full picture' – but is something to be shared, as we all share the same sun-light, the original creator of all the colours.

Can Environmental Use of Colour be Beneficial in Increasing Work Efficiency?

If Colour Harmony is skilfully designed into work-space, then this can produce the most astonishing, positive, results. Work efficiency and productivity improve when carried out in an environment which takes into account the effects of colour in interior design. The end result could be a service to both groups of people, the workforce and the management. Both can gain if colour is used widely by an experienced consultant – and both can loose in a badly coloured environment. For instance, in a red room people move more quickly, work faster, so it could seem that productivity should be increased. However, red will also cause the people working there to be more stressed, more irritable, slap-dash, more accident prone, so that the number of errors made also increases. There will also undoubtedly be more ill health amongst workers in the mid-to-long-term; more headaches, more blood pressure problems.

Is there a Non-Physical State of Colour which is not as yet, Measurable?

Our experience of Colour is directly linked with the conditions of life on this planet. We have air, gravity, and magnetism – creating conditions which are probably different from any other galactic environment, also our own eyes which function within these conditions. Hence, we may assume that colour can appear in very different modes in different atmospheres.

There may be, even on this planet, a pre-physical state of colour which may be linked to a field almost too fine to be measured by our present instruments. Dr. Walter Kilner around 1900, produced the Kilner Screen which showed colour immediately around and a little way beyond people's physical bodies. Kirlian photography, using high voltage electricity, also shows some of this non-manifest colour. Some people, and many children, before the age of six years, are conscious of these pre-manifest colours. In para-normal terms these colours are called an "Aura."

How Can we all Benefit from the Use of Colour?

It seems very important that we should become much more aware of colour than most of us are at present. With wise use and recognition of Colour and Illumination in our everyday lives, we can create a more harmonious and healthy environment for all. We should become more aware of our feeling responses to colour and learn to trust our intuitive senses before too many people suffer needlessly.

Illumination and Colour in Infant and Primary Schools

Do you remember that when we were small we all liked to play in corners and under tables, and if available in small caves and "Wendy-houses"? Twilight and even every little light was nicer than the broad daylight or the bright lamps which would show up our shortcomings, our incomplete states. All children like to hide, the opportunities to do so are very comfortable as the psyche of a child is a very shy entity. Children are beings of the twilight under which they find a very deep down feeling of protection. This protection is not given by darkness that removes all spatial concepts, nor by a brilliance which exposes all that which a child cannot as yet do "right"! Where do we learn that "right" doing? – In the protection of carefully chosen space, and colours which offer a deep psychological protection. During infancy the reds and the oranges combined with turquoises and blues contrast gently when used in their correct distribution in the child's environment.

The warmer range of the spectrum, excluding sharp yellows, are preferred in accordance with the child's needs to become more and more integrated with the physical world into which it has now been set. So the turquoises should be gentle, best chosen for curtains, cushions and any soft surface; also there can be blue, again soft, used as an addition or as an alternative colour instead of turquoise.

The Bedouins in the northern regions of Africa paint the inside of animal shelters light blue. It is the colour that works against fear and the absence of fear in itself is a protection against beasts of prey. It seems that the child finds much help when the inside of small places are of that light blue. Softness goes with gentle pastel colours. Hard walls, surfaces and other structures stand out as orientation in the stronger reds and oranges.

In a later stage of young people's lives, at the top of their senior school life this may well be reversed. It is in our view very bad to generalise, but it is an overall guideline.

Nothing can actually replace the Seminar where experience is shared and a good Lecturer is able to draw out of the audience present questions which will not arise in any other form.

It is important in the school-room environment to use colours as orientating factors. Children to a greater degree than adults (and in adults more women than men) are often very colour sensitive. A great deal of thought must go into the design and use of colours. Our present education spends a great deal of effort on the Scientific–Mathematical side of the children's talents.

The next important issue is physical education, games and sport. It is known that in the science area the blue tones support this branch of education, and that in the gymnasium the reds and oranges enhance the actual physical activities of the youngsters.

Children, before they read and write, have a very acute sense of orientating themselves with colour. A school could use this to help foster security in infants who are still in the pre-reading stages. If we wish to make the most of this, we could stick a colour, or even paint this colour on a large part of their desk or table. Each child individually can have its own place and its own colour. Children at that age should not be asked to make choices, this can only come later out of security absorbed through good guidance.

In order that such classroom remains in "one piece' it is important to follow the spectrum sequence which ends up with say twenty-four different shades of the reds to the violets. Even mentally handicapped children can differentiate safely and accurately between 5–9 different reds, greens, blues (7+2−2); this is a very interesting area of numbers in more than the one specific area as applied here. Keep the colours clear but not too harsh, nor should they be toned down with greys or browns. Colours of the latter type do not belong to that age.

Colours carefully applied fill an incredible gap in our educational system. As already mentioned above, the present system really ignores the child who lives actually between the intellect and the physical activities. It is there that the psyche has its 'play' – its blossoming or wilting can be manipulated by the use of environmental impressions, and none are as strong as colour.

Form, Sound, Colour and Healing

Just as we are drawn to listen more accutely to sounds which are gentle, so pastel colours cause us to sharpen our perception. This is specially so in young children, they are mostly judged by and subjected to adults' assumptions.

At the Kuwait Institute for Scientific Research (KISR), where I am a Consultant for Educational space, we actually worked with Staff and children for many months.

Much of the above has been experienced by the Research team, and so much more still needs to be done. To see the environment as the infant sees it is not an easy task for the intellectually thinking adult. The best training to obtain a view as the child has it, is actually working with handicapped children of both mental and physical disabilities; there we are forced almost to dive down into the concepts which are made by the child. I refer here to the excellent paper by Kenneth Bayes* much of which applies to the so called normal child.

These are very general guidelines which need to be viewed in very great detail when one is faced with a brief for a school, or just one classroom. There should be very careful and time absorbing preparations, research on the spot, and most important — the writing of the brief, which can then be correctly interpreted by the craftsman in charge.

The other most important area is the actual illumination. There is no excuse these days to have the bare and shocking off/on switch fitted because our health is the most valuable item we have. To repair the damage done is so expensive that the fitting of dimmer switches is mere 'chicken feed' and the use of incandescent or the now available, flicker free fluorescent light is very cheap in comparison with the millions spent to repair damage suffered later.

Children are very light sensitive and the off/on switching of light not only causes an outer flickering of their eyelids, but also a shock which is relayed via the pituitary gland to the whole nervous system. Most children today are hyper-active and the effect of light fading slowly in and fading out has a most soothing effect. Low level light with task lighting where needed is the ideal.

*The therapeutic effect of Environment on emotionally disturbed and mentally subnormal children . . . Kenneth Bayes, FRIBA, FSIA, Centre for the Environment, London.

The changes which are possible by using a careful mixture of lights and the introduction of coloured filters (well chosen) can give the teacher facilities that will calm or liven up children, or set the scene for listening, music making and playing.

Yes, it's fancy, it's unusual, it may even be argued to be wasteful and unnecessary. We do not think so. It is in childhood where peace and deeper development for a fuller person is awakened. If we are to look forward to a better future then the influences of both colour and illumination upon the human person have to be a decisive tool to bring out the positive potentials which lie latent in the child.

31st January 1984

Colour Illumination and Human Sight in Relation to Health

Introduction

From the time of the Cave-men onwards, man has sought to have some control over the natural rhythms of nature through the use of light.

We have progressed from the primitive fire, through the oil lamps and candles of early civilization, to the gas lamp, and then made a sudden tremendous leap forward with the invention of the incandescent lamp by Thomas Edison at the end of the last century. Another big step was taken in 1935 when Dr. Eng. Hans Heitler discovered the fluorescent light.

Suddenly man has been given nearly unlimited choice as to how much or how little light he wishes to have but we seem to be in pursuit of stronger and cheaper illumination without considering either the quality of this light or the effect it has on the nervous system.

This report is an attempt to briefly discuss some of the known effects of light on human beings.

Form, Sound, Colour and Healing

General Effects of Light

1. Illumination is increasingly recognised as one of the major contributors to human well-being since Bio-chemistry discovered in recent years what we at Hygeia Studios have long known – 'The human person is as light-sensitive as any plant' and every effort that is made for either the betterment or the worsening of the physical, mental or emotional state of a human being is largely subject to illumination. Where the betterment of human health is sought, then natural should be used as much as possible.

2. It is of great importance to deepen ones practical knowledge of the effects of lights when one is concerned with people whose nervous system is not functioning at the accepted 'normal' level – such people may be permanently epileptic, or mentally disabled, or they may be one of a great number of people who at sometime in their life, need psychiatric nursing in order to cope with the nervous stresses and strains of 'normal' living. The ever increasing marketing of anti-stress methods suggests that what is said here could apply to the majority of people today. Also, we are convinced through many years of direct experience with these people, that the nervous tension in a physically handicapped person is at a comparatively high level, and therefore the tranquility which arises from using the approach to illumination advocated in this report, is an essential part in any effort to create a better life for these people.

3. The proportion and distribution of window space in relation to well-being was well known by the Classical Architects but their ideals have been much altered. Shade and light raise people's awareness levels by presenting them with the opportunity of making a conscious choice. Nowadays there is unfortunately not always a choice; with so many buildings being designed with clear glass walls and no shade we seem to have come to an area which needs re-appraising.

4. There must be access for everyone during the daytime to the experience of clear unadulterated daylight, (preferably also to sunshine). The human eye needs this, and in blind people it can be said the whole person, as the cells of the skin have to compensate for the deficient or absent cells of the eyes. Without this experience of daylight many people who are borderline

depressive cases quickly experience a worsening of their conditions. Any area which prevents this, such as smoked glass, and windowless offices, schools etc., must also make provision for access to natural daylight if a balanced, healthy human being is to be created or maintained. Exclusion from this natural light environment can lead to a weakening or worsening of health patterns.

Artificial Illumination

Artificial illumination even at its best, is not a complete substitute for daylight, if one hopes to remain in good health. However, there is a vast difference between good, indifferent, and really bad artificial light. We do have some control over our state of well-being when using artificial illumination.

It is not generally known that the colour of a light has an effect on humans. The most frequently used street illumination is split into two main categories: Sodium vapour (red spectrum) and Mercury vapour (blue spectrum). The normal tungsten filament household lamp, although much closer to 'white' light, still has a fairly large incidence of the red spectrum. However, for the quality of its light, it is still the best illumination so far available, unless one used what is here described as electronically balasted fittings,* Full Spectrum Fluorescent light (known as True-Light) or the Pure Light Lamp (manufactured by Hygeia Manufacturing Limited).

Smoked Glass and Colour

Some limited research into the psychological effects of smoked glass for buildings, so frequently used nowadays, shows that it has a depressive effect on the human mind. People say "The sky is never clear outside." Really good illumination as described in the previous paragraph, can change this very considerably. It must be apparent that through this action many places could

---

* Available from Wye Estate, High Wycombe: unit IV, 'True Life'.

experience an increase in productivity through the avoidance of human errors and frequent sick leave. The general use of pigment colour in offices, industry, and schools must also be considered, as reflected and/or direct light is an important factor in the general behaviour of people.

Light and Communication

The amount of illumination has an incredible impact upon the communication levels of people. Very bright light will greatly discourage communication, while darkness changes the whole concept of communication, but this lies outside the scope of the present paper. These are of course, extreme situations; in between these two we have an infinite variety of different levels in communication influenced by the amount of illumination.

Harmony Response System

There is a very delicate inbuilt mechanism in the human response system which acts on a sub-conscious, automatic level, creating behaviour patterns. Within this subconscious level is contained the cell 'memory' of perfection, that is, the state of being at its most comfortable at any given moment. Even under very uncomfortable circumstances this perfect balance is sought; this is what makes an individual person move into the light, or out of the brilliant sunlight into shade. This is of course, also linked with our eye function, with the sense of sight. We must however, be clear that in using the sense of sight we are continually crossing the borderline between cell-memory and brain-memory. The brain reacts, through its conscious awareness of the present with the memory bank, and this is a point where we have free choice. We can either act through our intelligent awareness by making appropriate deductions from our environment, and recall learning from our past experiences, or we can use less logical factors which are frequently conditioned by our education, family or social background. It is through the actions of this memory bank which are semi-conscious/conscious that we make choices which are proved to be either right or wrong.

Colour and The Eye

The Human Eye, as it is a light-sensitive organ, can be greatly benefited by good use of environmental colour, which will reflect to the eye changes of light that can prevent the eyesight from losing its life energy. In extreme cases, where for a prolonged period the eye focus is kept at a static level, we have a situation with a high potential for eye strain and general tiredness. For instance, these may be people whose eye focus is fixed for a long time on an object which neither varies in focal distance nor colour.

Ways and Means

Hygeia Studios have found in their research that there are several ways in which such detrimental effects can not only be alleviated, but can also be improved. Whilst normal work is continued a therapy can be introduced via mobile illumination levels and colour changes.

Let us consider Mobile illumination – Firstly, we can now have low level general illumination; then secondly, provide each individual's work area with a task light. If this light is a good substitute for daylight, and not distorted by the usual artificial illumination colours, and if it is also controllable by its individual dimmer switch, then people are given the opportunity to change the tension of their eye muscles. This tension is created by the impact of light upon the retina. The rods and cones which are within the retina must be kept mobile, as static positions cause tiredness, known as 'eye-strain' in normal language.

We must now consider in some detail what effect different colours have on the eye as a whole.

Change of Focus Through Colour

If we lay a red filter over the page of a book we find that the focusing of the eye takes place behind the retina, making the page[1] look nearer to us, whereas by placing a blue filter over the page the focusing changes to in front of the retina, and the page looks further away. Green is the only colour that is actually focused on the retina, and this provides a mid-point between the two extremes.

On this knowledge is based our Eye Strengthening Chart which[1] we have developed in the course of our research, and the habit of publishing our books as often as possible on several different colours of tinted paper. Printing on tinted paper is not just some 'fancy' idea, for as you change from one colour to another the muscles of the retina alter their tension. With this method, reading is not as tiring on the eyes; it give them a mobility which is very beneficial.

We recommend that when reading on one-colour paper you give your eyes an occasional rest by looking at a blue, then at a red surface – possibly a wall colour or a furnishing colour. Do this for maybe fifteen seconds each, and you should be able to read without the usual eye-strain.

One of the recent causes of increasing eye-strain is the use of Visual Display Units (V.D.U.). If we are to avoid real damage to eyes we should be able to provide alternative colours for the viewing; we suggest again a red and a blue filter which can change regularly the colour of the characters being read by the operator. Potentially these ideas can have a great influence on health and eyesight. We must consider not only reflected decor colours but remember that coloured light is enormously important because the light carries the colour right into our bodies. We are the recipients of that energy, and we must consider what effects coloured illumination has on people's cell structure. What effect does coloured illumination have on the cell structure of any living organism?[4] To consider the extremes of red and blue: Red will always cause a slight constricting of the cell size. This is demonstrated by blood pressure which is raised a little by a person's exposure to red. An analogy can be made with water flowing through a pipe; more pressure is needed to force the same amount of water in the same time, through a small pipe than through a larger one. Under exposure to blue light, cells expand slightly and blood pressure is reduced. Decor and clothing are both capable of producing this effect, but when light is used the difference is much more strongly marked.

Eye Balancing

Hygeia Research has also discovered some very useful ways of using colour in cases where people suffer from a lazy eye, or from one eye being strong and the other weak. For instance, we may design spectacles which have a dark (violet) filter for one eye, and a light (yellow) filter for the other, instead of the normal lens.[3] The strong dominant eye will be protected from overstrain by using the dark filter, and the lazy eye will be encouraged to become more active by using the light filter. If these spectacles are worn for a while regularly each day an improvement will occur in the weak eye, and the stronger eye will not be so tired.

Illumination Methods

Any artificial lighting, if it is to be beneficial, must clearly take account of two main factors:

(a) The colour of that lighting (most illuminations has a high incidence of the red spectrum). So little has been taught about this subject that many mistakes are made.
(b) The steadiness or the evenness of light. This depends on the incandescent material in the light. All tungsten, or mineral based filaments provide what we would call a stable illumination due to their thermal inertia.

Illumination changes its quality as soon as we change from the mineral (dense) element to gas (vapour) as used in fluorescent lighting. The gas is too insubstantial to remain glowing constantly through the cycles of the AC (mains) current, and the result is a 100 × second flicker which some people are consciously aware of. The remainder of the population experience this at a subliminal level, but it can still cause eyestrain, irritation, headaches etc., In fact, the inventor of the fluorescent lamp, Dr. Hans Heitler, considered it to be a cheap light for emergency (wartime) use only, knowing that it could in long term use, be a health hazard. When a fault occurs in these lamps and they flicker at a very slow rate, the tension and annoyance, therefore health risk, is greatly increased.

In our view it is not enough to consider only the colour hue of fluorescent tubes, although this has some effect.

To avoid nervousness and general tension all vapour based illumination must be treated with the now available Solux Electronically ballasted fittings, which virtually change the AC current into DC, thus eliminating the on-off flicker. When this is done, and we also incorporate the work of Dr. J. Ott who experimented with plants and illumination levels in schools, and from the results of this developed the full spectrum fluorescent tubes (also known as True-light), will we have as near as possible, healthy illumination.

Conclusion

From the evidence it is our firm belief from our research results so far, that it must only be a matter of time and the methodical corrolation of further research here, before colour both pigment and illumination as well as the quality and quantity of light, can be so harnessed that they will be beneficial to the preservation of human eye-sight. Furthermore, we are convinced that coloured lights can be used to help in the cure of illness, and that colour should become a supplementary therapy available to all who can benefit from such treatment. There is a need to promote and to encourage much research which must then be applied.[4]

Theo Gimbel D.C.E.
Member of the Light and Health
Research Council. (MLHRC)

---

[1] Such as either 'Leefilters' No. 153 Pale salmon or 'Cinemoid' No. 10 Middle Rose. (The two are not identical but provide a choice, the latter having a little more blue in it.) For red 'Leefilter' No. 117 Steel-blue, or 'Cinemoid' No. 40 pale blue for blue.
[2] For blue BS 18 E51. For red BS 01 E53.
[3] The degree of the hues of these filters cannot be fixed for a general use as it varies from client to client.
[4] *Growing Plants under Colour*, (Daylight) – a Hygeia Publication. Theo Gimbel, 1974. Also in *Healing Through Colour*, The C. W. Daniel Co., 1980, p. 162.

Evidence of Colour-Influence upon Chemical and Biological Cell Structure

According to the physical and bio-chemical laws all biological structure can be made to change through circumstances of temperature, illumination, and the passing of time.

These are just the most obvious influences which are understood by most people today.

We are concerned here with the influences which can be effected by illumination, such as exposure to bright lights. This consistently over days, weeks, and months, will have an ageing (maturing) influence upon plants, animals, and humans – darkness has a rejuvenating effect.

Research with plants and animals remains fairly consistent, whereas with humans we are experiencing an important overriding factor: Consciousness and the capacity to think, which we now know can alter the outcome of any exposure and/or treatment.

The second most important law is that the most mobile, sensitive structures are also the most vulnerable cells.[1]

The research carried out since 1968 at Hygeia Studios has produced for us a very specialised branch of bio-chemical structure. This not only links this to light (illumination) but also to the very finely qualified illumination.

There is ample evidence to support the fact that red light increases blood pressure and blue light reduces it. However, what are the facts behind this sudden change through coloured lights?

(a) The vibration per second of red is slower than that of blue (violet) 4.5×10^{14} = red, 7.6×10^{14} = blue violet.
(b) Any biological structure contracts under red and expands under blue. Hence red creates a tight packing structure, and blue a loose packing structure.

This means in ordinary practical terms, that our entire bodies shrink when subjected to red, and expands when exposed to blue light, (illumination).

Starting with very simple experiments[2], we investigated the change in blood pressure in people when subjected to red and then to blue light. Red consistently increased blood pressure (and speeded up breathing), whilst blue decreased blood pressure (and slowed down breathing).

Returning to the research of Dr. W. Kelley, the human body has a scale of very sensitive to rather less sensitive cells. Those which are the most mobile are embryonic and continually change from virgin structures to inverted cell structures. They are also very easily influenced by coloured illumination.

All plant, animal, and human beings obey the law of development and are all light sensitive. The qualified light i.e. coloured has in recent years become a matter of increasing concern to people from all walks of life. Maybe the first attention to this came from the most alarming results of indiscriminate use of colour and strobe lights in discotheques. From there it is a small step to the question of general health in people who see very little daylight.

Green light can influence, and as it were, dissolve the cells of living structures in accordance with their sensitivity degree.

So we have already three colours which are known to have an influence over the cell behaviour.

Colour has been used to verify many physical and optical measurements and we are certain that its many spectral shades can be used to improve the wellbeing, or for that matter influence negatively, the health of plants, animals, and humans.

Degrees of light both in quantity and quality are responsible for a balanced state of health, it is only a matter of time and resources, before all the qualities of colour (mostly of illumination) exposure will be known to have quite accurately predictable influences on the health of the body of humans.

The many obvious benefits of colour are also discussed in the recent paper: *Colour and Illumination and Human Sight in Relation to Health.*[3]

Many of the benefits of colour both psychologically and physiologically are still subject to much testing and research. However, the evidence to hand at present suggests that much of the findings will be substantiated in the near future. The addition of colour as a supplementary therapy will become one of the other items to which the Prince of Wales said: "What is taken for today's unorthodoxy is probably going to be tomorrow's convention."[4]

Observation Report on Human Reactions to Coloured Illumination

By Theo Gimbel
Director of Research

Since 1956 it has been observed by me that certain reactions and behaviour changes take place when people (including children) are exposed to coloured light.

Then, and even now, one can use very simple and inexpensive equipment; and the best results are obtained when using daylight. This, however, requires very elaborate black-out facilities for any one room used for this work.

Gradually over the last 20 years much research has revealed that electric light does have a use in this; and one can simplify matters for the colour exposures.

We have here observed that not only good results are available, but that quite definite precautions and a careful training is needed for the constructive use of colour, if we suggest this as one of the alternative but rather, say, supporting therapies, for the medical work.

Thus, in the training of what we like to refer to here as Colour Therapists, one cannot afford to be haphazard or to just have a vague idea as to how to set about this Therapy. Ultimately it is a discipline which we must use like any other therapy.

In student volunteers, of whom we have had many, it has been quite clearly observed that the benefit is increased if we use a restricted and carefully selected amount of light and colour.

---

[1] D. Med. William Kelley BS, BA, MS, DDS.
[2] *Growing Plants under Colour (daylight)* Theo Gimbel DCE, MIACT, MLHRC.
[3] Theo Gimbel, Hygeia Publications, October 1983.
[4] The Prince of Wales *The Times*, 16 December 1982

A quite definite increase of vitality and blood pressure, has been clearly observed when volunteers in the research have been exposed to red light (100 watt per 37.5 cub. yards).

Conversely, if exposed to blue light (100 watt, same space), a very considerable drop in blood pressure has been noticed.

For Red we used: No. 16.

For Blue we used: No. 19 (Rank Strand Electric: Cinemoid Filters).

The exact wavelength can, of course, be measured with an adequate instrument. (This Establishment has not had the funds to acquire one.)

A list of colours used by us is given here:

> Red: No. 6 (Primary Red)
> Orange: No. 35 (Deep Golden Amber)
> Yellow: No. 1 (Yellow)
> Green: No. 39 (Primary Green)
> Turquoise: No. 16 (Blue Green)
> Blue: No. 19 (Dark Blue)
> Violet: No. 25 (Purple)
> Magenta: No. 13 (Magenta)

If we used more than 3 colours in any one 30 minute exposure, the result was, in 73% cases, uneasiness and arousal – to the extent that sleeplessness ensued for up to the next 48 hours.

However, if any three colours, of which one was always Blue, have been used, no complaints were made.

Over the years we have come to use very exact timing, which has its own rhythms in natural space and time measurements.[1] This again has produced very extraordinary results.

Colours, like most other environmental experiences, come in complementary sets of two. So, using the above 8 colours, we have started to use these as described in the handout: *Treatment Rhythms for Colour Therapy*.[2]

The next stage we asked ourselves, was – is it of any special significance if we use square openings, round openings (apertures) to show the light? Here we came to use some new ideas which have proved successful, and we found it relevant

---

[1] Golden mean 1.6181 or $\sqrt{\frac{5+1}{2}}$

[2] See *Healing Through Colour* page 136 onwards.

whether a Red colour is projected through a round or a triangular opening but has either supporting or subtracting influences.

Thus we have developed designs which change the grid of light in sympathy with the colour used. It has become quite clear here that we do have to deal with responses which are not from the eyes but from the nerve ends of the skin of our volunteers.

It appears that the 'density' of a particular colour is picked up by the nerve ends and 'marries' with the 'chemical sheath' at the body surface. It further seems as if a message is then received from this area and communicated to all vessels and glands to which each body reacts.*

May I apologise for my own terminology – as I am not a medically trained person, I must resort to some more general language.

All our pilot schemes can be carried out by any person sufficiently clear in the comprehension of time, order and rhythm – and careful keeping of notes.

Positive Changes

There are seven steps which are to be considered when a human being is desirous to incarnate.

This soul (I) 'looks' as it were 'down' to overshadow the two already incarnate souls who seek each other and often know that this was a guided meeting.

The love-making which can be from a purely sexual event to the most enlightened and spiritually prepared ceremony leads to conception (II). On the average there are forty hours between love-making and conception (forty weeks in the womb). This number can be further enlarged upon, (see the Colour Circle Nos 18 & 21).[1]

The cells which build the embryo are here called EC. Again forty hours before birth there is a calcium process which produces the Virgin cell (VC) and from this moment onwards the

---

*All our volunteers have been advised always to wear white clothes when working with colour.

Form, Sound, Colour and Healing

development of the body is a continual building of virgin cells which must follow the path of an inversion (IC) and this enables the cell to become useful in the growing and renewal of the body so that on the average 7 + 2 − 2 years all cells are replaced. The last step is to let the cell go to become earth as it falls off the skin (hair, etc.), at the rate of a few billions per day.[2]

This concludes plan A.

If in the path of life the incarnated soul is faced with major blocks which undermine the chances to resolve problems which block the way which this soul wishes to go, and in the emotional, mental, and physical vision there are no new ways open, the plan B can appear to be followed. The speed at which this happens

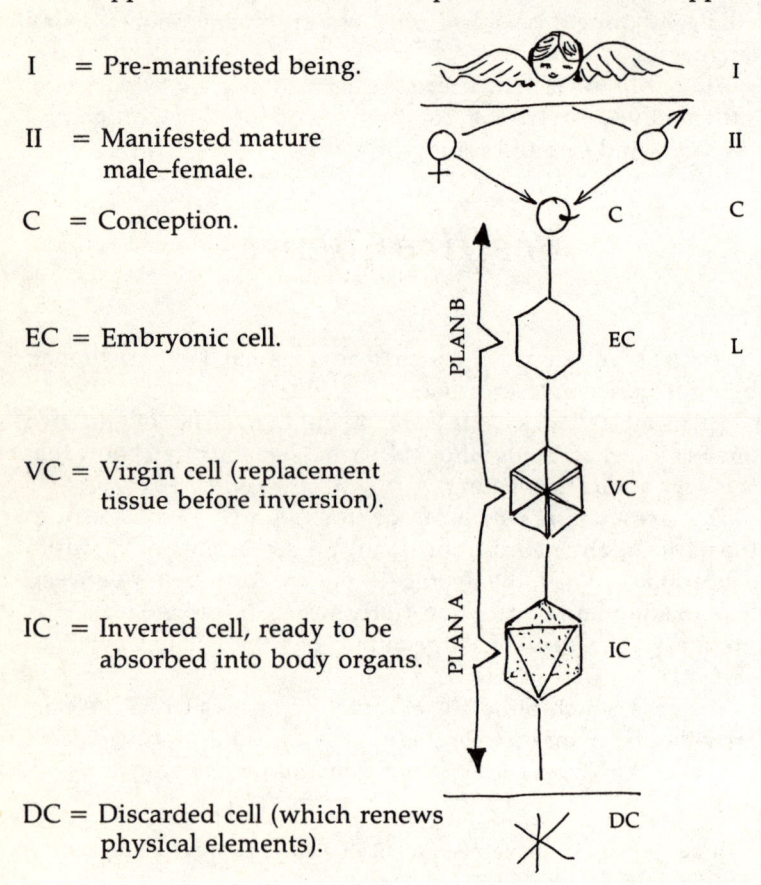

I = Pre-manifested being.

II = Manifested mature male–female.

C = Conception.

EC = Embryonic cell.

VC = Virgin cell (replacement tissue before inversion).

IC = Inverted cell, ready to be absorbed into body organs.

DC = Discarded cell (which renews physical elements).

depends very much on the battles which are fought within the soul. The complexity to which this plan B is followed can be so different in timing and in its whole 'ups and downs' that there are very few known rules. However, one of the rules most recently found is that of the patient involved therapy. This means to understand in principle what is happening. According to Professor Christopher Marjorie (Australia) the thinking method and the acceptance of counselling by those who have a clear insight into the nature of this plan B has yielded unprecedented success to the point that two thirds of patients can be so successfully counselled that operations become unnecessary.

Plan A can be very quickly restarted. I have known that within 48 hours malignant cells have reverted into benign, and over some period of time sometimes even years, the conscious, working on the body, the person involved managed to eliminate the benign cells and cope with a new found health style; active support of the instrument (the body) with a feeling to be in command to conduct his/her own affairs and not only to find this in itself a path never trodden before, but also the rekindling of old ways, which without this challenge, would have been dead.

The actual reversal of this plan A is as real as facts and physics in space and time. Often very deep subconsciously from VC the deep longing comes as much as to say: "I want to go back to where I came from", but not knowing the path, either way to come or go in or out of this manifestation, is of no help. Not until that is clearer and a basic principle can be found to conduct this being alive as a personal responsibility, will there arise the real hope of being in charge.

Lastly, if a piece of steel can be altered drastically by a change from non-magnetic to magnetic, which needs the re-arrangement of the molecular structure, then why cannot a human being change the infinitely more sensitive biology within?

Theo Gimbel, June 1983

---

1 Ascension Day.
2 "Supernature" Lyall Watson.

"The Sculptor"

There was a Sculptor, a very skilled and beautiful person. She had a large garden. The garden contained so many beautiful areas and all of these areas were visited often time and again, but there were one or two areas which she had almost forgotten about and she found herself wondering whether one or the other area in that beautiful garden would be a spot where she could work. So, she took with her some tools and a lump of clay and went through the garden. When she arrived at a spot which she had so long forgotten, she found it rather obscured with weeds and growth so that was not at all a garden. So she put down her tools and her clay and made herself some space in that apparent wilderness. Then she made a circle of protection and she gave that circle the greatest of care around the area that she had now cleared. The weeds and growth that she had cut away she took into another part of the garden where she usually burnt all the things that were supposed to become fruitful earth for the rest of the garden plants. Then having done that, she felt that there was a beautiful clear space made, and swept the part where she was now going to set up her sculpture. She took some clay and her tools and made a beautiful place right in the middle of this circle that she had made and she sat down; but before she began to work she sat quietly and contemplated about what the sculpture should become, for she had no fixed idea at this moment of how it should be formed.

In her mind she looked around the whole of her inner garden, she visited every part, and she felt that every part had something else to say. Her head was like the most wonderful crystal. It was also part of the ground where one could actually look out, in fact, she discovered that she was never so clear about it. She could see the whole of the garden, right to the very end by the gate to that private garden, and she wondered. And then, she did not know exactly what to do with this piece of clay which she had brought, she just let her hands be guided, and she started to mould it letting her hands go free. It was not easy to do, but she felt that her hands were guided and so she forgot about the long, long time that she had now been sculpting and when she looked again she stood back from the work she had done, and found herself with this wonderful feeling that although her head could have thought of many, many special things, her own hands had been guided to mould a sculpture that she herself could not have known; could she have perceived it in her head?

It had a wonderful upright stillness as it stood there like something that was sure of itself, and then it seemed as if the form suggested that it might go on and on beyond the actual crystal sculpture, and that it had been rooted very deeply to the earth. As she walked around it, looking from side to side, she realised that there was also a most extra-ordinary balance from right to left, and left to right, and there was a wonderful way in which this balance kept itself in harmony with the very upright feeling of the sculpture. So she was pleased, and she walked around a little bit more and saw it from yet another side. Then suddenly she realised it was as if it wanted to go on a journey. It is a feeling as if it had come from another part of the garden and that it wanted to go far beyond to another part of the garden that it had not seen, and this third energy in that sculpture became a very wonderful movement, the uprightness, the balance and the will to go. She hardly dared to touch the sculpture any longer because she felt she had achieved something, as if her hands had been guided by angels. Something that she herself could never have dreamt up, she herself could never have managed it.

So with great respect and great care she just made it that much more beautiful, finishing off the somewhat unfinished parts, and spent a long time on it. By now several days had passed and she went every day to that new place which was prepared in the garden to do a little more on the sculpture, and just at that very moment when she was beginning to make the last touches, she felt as if there was a very beautiful feeling beside her, giving her support.

This feeling also said "You can be proud of what you have achieved, you listened and you felt into spaces that are not normally trodden by all people; I called and you listened, and you touched into fields of my own energy, therefore you have become a friend of mine, we understand each other well. Therefore I want you to know that you can always ask me, your guide, questions that you will be asking as we go on our journey together.

Form, Sound, Colour and Healing

So you are not alone, you are accompanied, and that company which we share with each other, is going to be there for ever. I knew you long, long ago when you had not come onto this earth and I knew that one day you would have to find me. At times it was almost painful for me to see you not wanting to find me, but I knew also that you must be free, without any demands, and I gave you undemanding and unlimited love, and with that I hoped that you could also learn to absorb that undemanded and unlimited love so that we could through the understanding we have, always be friends together – in joy, in sorrow, in laughter, and in tears we are not separated."

So the beautiful lady sat in that space which she had made herself for quite a long time, and consciously thought about what a beautiful guide she had seen. Then she went to the place which she usually preferred in the house; where there are books to enjoy, nice records to listen to, and she found her own freedom and peace. She did not feel that she was going to take up sculpturing anywhere else, having prepared that part of the garden, and it now became the centre of the garden; although it was far from being in the centre of the garden, it was a very important place. So she left the sculpture just there, and she found some stones with which she surrounded it so that it should not be disturbed by anyone.

She grew into a very fine artist and had many conversations with her guide who first revealed himself to her. She became aware that she could mould and fashion again, her creative spirit had awakened afresh, and with a very strong impulse.

Spoken for Anna S. when she had to wrestle with cancer during Colour Therapy –

Theo Gimbel
Brook House, Avening.

The Colour Composer

As a harmoniser to restore balance and equilibrium to the viewer.

The origin of this instrument has been to achieve through music

A Threefold Approach to a Patient – Involved Therapy

colour from and movement the above mentioned benefits. The concepts are that colour is a very fine and gentle media which can produce harmony and peace in those who are subjected to this influence.

We use classical music, specially selected to be suitable for an emotional, mental, and psychological re-alignment.

It is of importance to the human being what kind of forms are being made available to the viewer. Research has led us to understand the impact of such symbols as the basic design of a valley that when you go down one side of the mountain you go up the other side and that a smile of contentment is brought into this form. Mathematically this is known as the even order curve a number 2, 4, 6 etc., curve. It is also the form of the chalice, the container, protection and the symbol of life; fullness and sustenance. Quite a difference, incomplete and most unsatisfactory energy is the uneven number curve 3, 5, 7 etc., Hopelessness, despair, emptiness, loss depression, these are the general feelings aroused by this curve.

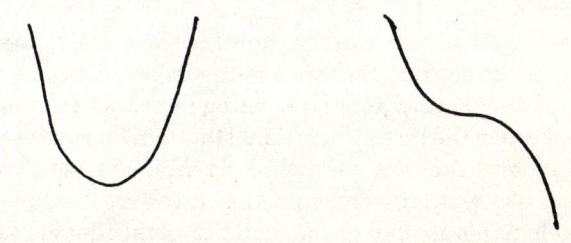

We are showing an incomplete and non-compensatory form element. It is a challenge, frequently too strong for some people.

Provided we make the top left side into a starting point, its there where out of the darkness, the unknown, the original all appear our first thoughts. The idea, the concept is often so very much the perfect, absolutely beautiful. Artists may well know this when first ideas are conceived. From there we now try and integrate this idea; little by little we are made aware that we are unable to bring this idea into reality, that we are finding painful frustration, material, skill, techniques, not forgetting patience, are lacking – we are left in a despair, sad, unfulfilled . . .

There arises the question, how on earth do we nevertheless create? What is there to give us the help which we need?

As we descend into the zero point we are letting the created

Form, Sound, Colour and Healing

moment stand apart from us, stand without this creator's joy an objectivity, neither sad nor elevated perseverance and progress

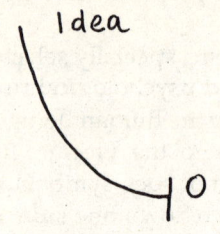

must be made in spite of the zero point we have the tendency to resurrect, go up to the other side of the valley.

In the efforts to bring down into being our idea, the concept of ideal, the perfect the beautiful original thought has in a way died in us. So what makes it nevertheless possible to have a creation go forward – upward towards this ideal idea? We need to look at what the elements are that go into that loss of the idea at the point zero. What is happening to the creator this being who in the days of innocence in the days of lack of self criticism and childlike folly lost so much? Where does the resurrection appear from when in the zero point we nevertheless go on? How do we find the

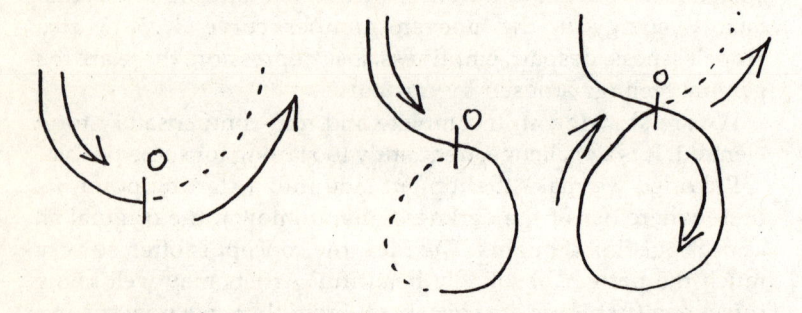

courage, the energy, the hope, the drive? you name it! – From the days of innocence when many things just disappeared and were apparently lost to us in the subconscious, silently a hitherto unobserved path was trodden by our super-subconscious unawares of the hustle and bustle of the common day. In this soul-maturing underworld our deep, sacred self walked with the lost perfection through this other darkness and reach zero from left below. We seem to bring experience into this point zero, that transforms itself into courage to let the idea rise within us in spite of the apparent death. Now we are helped to manifest this idea. The path becomes confirmed and we are led to see not only the tentative possibility but also the fulfilment as the confirmation reaches the soul of the creator – artist as consciousness on creating. In this hidden darkness an inner glow of comfort is rising in the soul and a certain joy of understanding which makes out of the dilemma a sudden insight; how necessary it was to loose in order to find. Now all that was previously lost refinds itself and becomes the tremendous power to create and bring the ideal idea to expression. With this we can now courageously go and manifest the fruits of our labours. But as we arrive at this right upward swing we behold the most glorious image of completion.

There is an awareness, the recognition of our creative path, which rises and takes us, all of us, yes, even the sad memories, the anger, the regrets, and the losses, and the realising out point, which was zero, now to be that point of creation because we can by that make a harmony, a holy, all out of the 'below' and marry the heavens to the earth. The sudden awareness which comes to our understanding; yes, it is the symbol of infinity, the eternal leminscate, the double circle which has the form of redemption, the form of completing the two cycles on an ever expanding new level with the old well-known symbols. Observe carefully seeing this now in the eternity pattern; World without end and weaving the everlasting renewal, re-birth of the idea as an ideal.

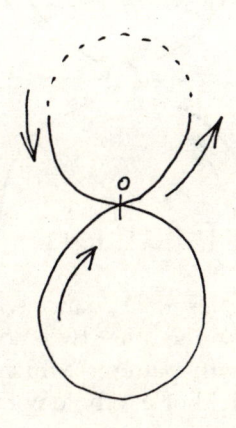

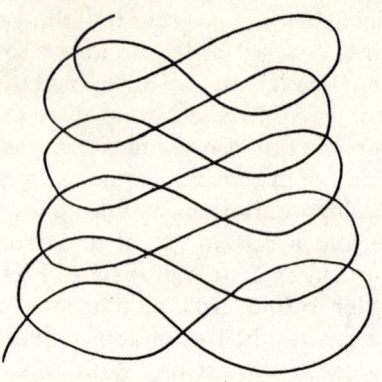

These are the principles which underly the forms, the now acceptable idea of the duality that serves the trinity of existence, the two who serve the third and that third is found when both energies rise and fall through zero. There are the deeper meanings of the polarity, the external complimentary energies found in her the woman, and in him the man. The logic (male) needs to die into zero so that the intuitive (feminine) can rise through zero and both are of the utmost need to this principle of what is, the purpose of communication.

Now we must see how we can raise this principle further into movement then into colour and bring this idea to completion in music.

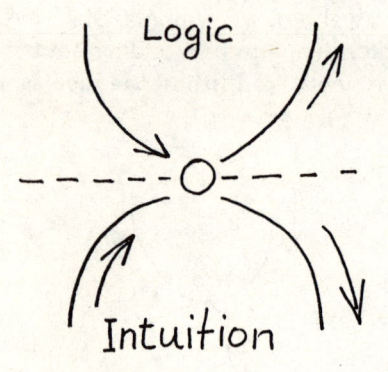

Let these two principles move, dance with each other and we will see how there arise the other two most important areas of human potential growth patterns which are needed to any development. In the field of psychology they are known as the

A Threefold Approach to a Patient – Involved Therapy

introvert and the extrovert, the concave and convex. As these two are allowed to play and move they go together dancing through all their various patterns at an ever extended cycle of renewal, introvert going through zero 0 and extrovert doing the same at opposite moments in time.

These states of existence are known as the manic-depressive personality (yellow) and the depessive personality (violet). We now begin to use colour which is the next step in the process to complete the idea of co-operation between the four parts which will complete the whole experience. As the forms move through zero colour at the moment is also at zero, now we can show the actual concepts used in this form element which gives rise to composing the colours to it.

By the use of two of the above forms we can create an ever self-renewing image which however has a stabilising factor built in by way of the determined, not vague, forms used.

Back projected lights, yellow, red and blue create coloured shadows onto a semi opaque screen. These lights are themselves mobile slowly rotating. The colours travel: blue at an outer circle, yellow at an intermediate circle, and red close to the centre. The three distances are measured in accordance to the golden mean or the fibonacci order of numbers; (3–5–8–13 etc.). The increased

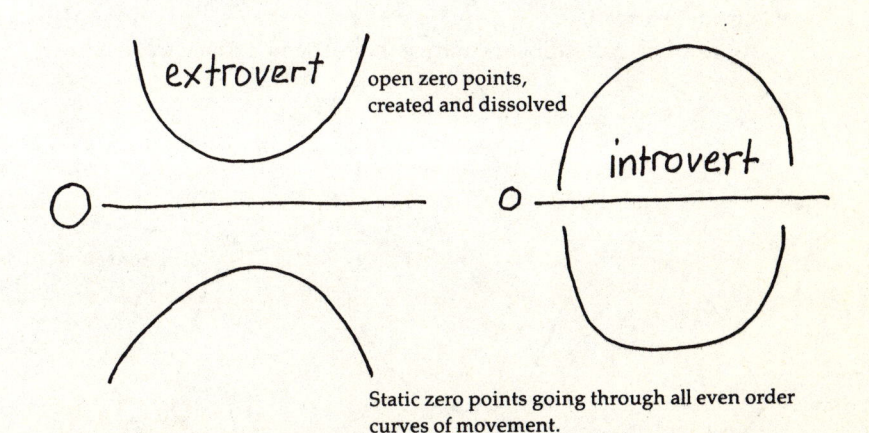

extrovert / open zero points, created and dissolved / *introvert*

Static zero points going through all even order curves of movement.

measure therefore is dark (no light) at centre point = 0, red light at 3, yellow at 5, and blue at 8. The proportions of these distances are in harmony with the human (and incidently all natural) growth patterns. This also creates the further additional harmony of the composers capacity.

Using these lights we can create, via dimming devices, an infinite and smooth variation of all rainbow colours – violet, orange, green, magenta, turquoise and all manner of variations are built into this colour display.

Finally to the music basically this can be live or recorded music. Orchestral pieces are most suitable and within this some compositions are most valuable as the colours, forms, and movement created bring up some most moving experiences to people. Some have stated that after an initial traumatic experience they then found their inner being brought into peace and harmony. Such things like stress and tension both mental and emotional have been brought to states of relaxation and calm inner feelings as well as the re-establishment of good and normalised behaviour patterns – obsessional ideas have been dissolved and minds set at ease. All in all it bears what we originally intended to achieve here.

We now have the hope to create, with the resources of research undertaken by our Associate Electronic Design Engineer Clifford Archer, the building of our colour composer, which can be linked to any record or cassette and individual colour. Form movements are made possible by the use of some very advanced electronic expertise.

Some of the composers which have been most effective in

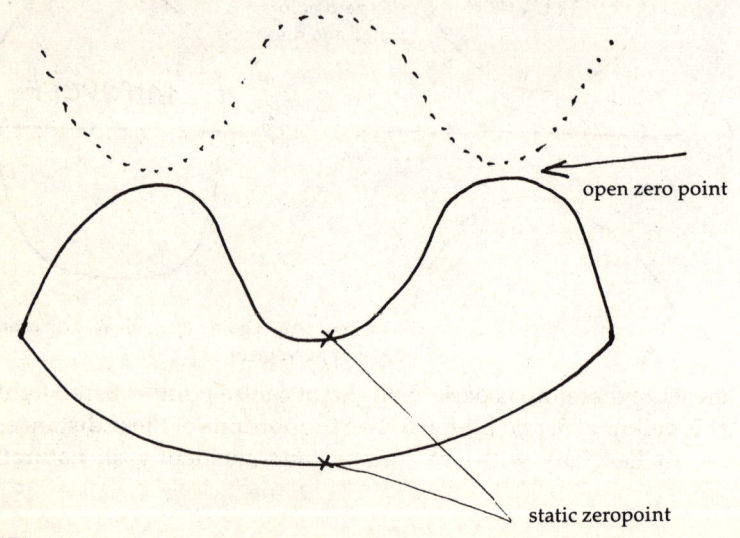

open zero point

static zeropoint

creating good results are Handel, Mozart, Beethoven, but especially J. S. Bach; in the music of Bach we find a natural concept of balance. This composer above all, has used music in its law linked to mathematics and finally for the restoration of balance. The effect is that while listening to his music the salt, sulphur, and mercury equilibrium is restored in the biological structures of plants, animals, and humans.

Bethesda
10.3.82
Theo Gimbel

Light as a way to Positive Health

Daylight is the natural birthright of all human beings; indeed it is the light which allows life to exist on this planet by way of photosynthesis in plants. It is gradually being revealed by many different researchers that light is of much more importance to us human beings than has previously been accepted, may be the next important thing after food.

Ever since Prometheus we have used fire as light, and since Edison we have it in little bottles, hanging from ceilings and walls. Real daylight cannot (yet) be copied, artificial light is however a necessary addition or substitution for it during some part of each day. Many of us have to spend much of each day under artificial illumination, and good lighting should be considered very important when designing our working, leisure or home space. Good light is (a) a steady light, and (b) gives off a colour which has many health benefits. These two factors have to go hand in hand to offer the very best illumination.

Vibrations are the rhythms of life. The heartbeat, respiration, eyeblinking are just the very coarse and obvious ones. Beyond these, both within the human person, as well as outside, are other rhythms, other vibrations, which are partly known and partly still to be found.

In music rhythms have been known and are used via the sense of hearing. When these rhythms/vibrations speed up, they reach the sense of sight; we no longer hear these but we see them. Sight and consciousness is much stimulated by light or light changes.

It is there that we have to make a study. It has become very well known that certain light flickers, or strobe lights can interfere with brain activity and with the normal functions of consciousness. Good, steady light promotes good thinking capacity; it also promotes a relaxed state of tension in the bio-chemical structures; it can very effectively reduce stress and the overstraining of eyesight. Bad lighting does the reverse.

Fluorescent light is very cheap to run, but is not a particularly steady light. By its nature, it has an obvious light rhythm. Incandescent light, by virtue of its thermal inertia, has a gentle curve, but the usual fluorescent light has a very aggressive wave pattern. This produces a flicker which is increasingly obvious at the tubes' connections as it ages.

It is, however, present even in new tubes, but is too fast for most people to be consciously aware of, though some are. However, the brain registers it subliminally, and the effect of this flicker is often to interfere with the central nervous system's control of the body. Much research, made possible through Electroencephalograph equipment (EEG) shows that this can be the cause of many of the problems attributed to fluorescent lighting – symptoms such as headaches, giddiness, loss of balance, eyestrain and feelings of sickness. Should the flicker slow down, therefore becoming more obvious, as the tube ages, then it can stimulate the brain into producing different wave patterns, some of which have even more undesirable results, such as triggering epileptic fits even in people with no previous history of them.

As well as the steadiness we also have to consider the colour of artificial lighting. Light alters the lens of our eyes and changes the rods and cones of the retina. It is less well known that it also changes the whole of the physical molecular structure of a person, and that this change is emphasized or decreased according to the colour of that light. Therefore, the different colour tones of artificial light should also be considered when choosing lighting. Dr. John Ott, in the USA, spent many years researching the best form of artificial light, and came up with a full spectrum tube which is the nearest equivalent to natural daylight yet available.

A Threefold Approach to a Patient – Involved Therapy

Ordinary illumination is usually giving off a yellow/red colour (tungsten and most fluorescents) or exceptionally a cold blue (north light fluorescents); both these encourage our eyes and molecular structure into an inflexible tension, from which there are many results, including eye-strain, and increased general tension and stress.

Hygeia Studios have, throughout years of research, been deeply concerned in creating artificial light at its very best, and we now have available lights that can be varied according to the state of well-being of each individual person, and also lights which reduce eyestrain and mental tensions.

The Pure Light Lamp is not just a desk lamp or decorative in your study, but it offers a very fine quality reading light with very great benefits to the eyes of the reader. There are NO colour distortions so you can enjoy textiles, illustrations and the natural colour of your friends faces, etc.

In the Colour Space Illuminator, the colour and level of illumination can be adjusted to give the amount of stimulation or relaxation required to help bring a person into balance with his natural rhythms.

The latest type of illumination to be introduced are our flicker free fluorescent fittings with full spectrum tubes.

These eliminate the bad effects of fluorescent lights by speeding up the electrical supply so that the flicker is eliminated. Also there is no hum or sound, and no sudden flashes of light as the fluorescent is switched on. We also recommend the use of full spectrum tubes which are as near as yet possible to natural daylight.

Through our study on the effects of light on the health patterns of people, we have developed our now well-known Colour Therapy as one of the supplementary treatments to aid health. The book *Healing Through Colour*, Theo Gimbel 1980, C. W. Daniel & Co, is an important book on the fundamental training of how to employ colour and light for health.

At last – A fluorescent Light that you can feel good with!

This light eliminates all the troubles normally associated with fluorescent lighting. No more tubes flickering above you. No more flashes as you switch on. No more hum or sound. (A specially designed inverter speeds up the electrical supply so that the flicker is eliminated.) And full spectrum tubes give you the advantages of normal daylight. Pure colour tones, no more distorted colours.

We have researched into the effects of light and colour on humans for many years, and this is the first fluorescent light fitting that we can recommend. Quality is never cheap, but the tubes have a life span many times longer than normal, and the savings that arise because the ill-effects on the central nervous system are no longer present are more than repaying your original investment.

General light wave patterns for contemporary lighting.

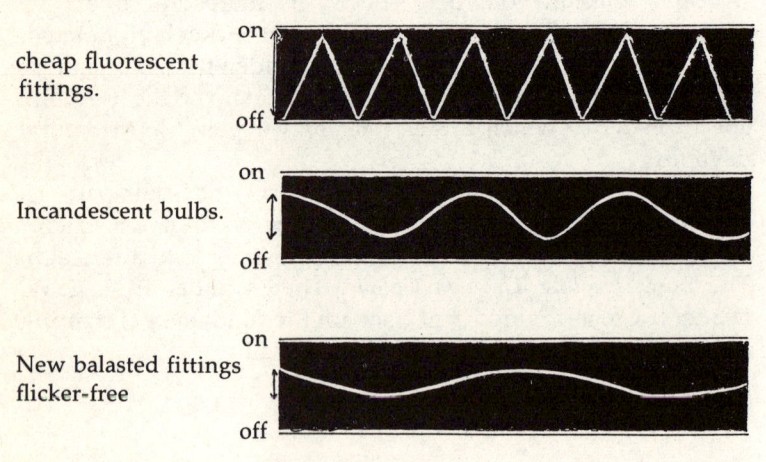

cheap fluorescent fittings.

Incandescent bulbs.

New balasted fittings flicker-free

Play, Consciousness and a Playground for Man

Education is a life process and therefore has neither beginning nor end.

Communication has a thousand ways in which it expresses itself. On such a line of the human path can be many significant areas which ought to be brought into education.

Is it not important that we start with the actual processes which are not only laws of this planet but also the laws of the universe?

If Rudolf Steiner has indeed helped humanity to break through into the new age and opened man's thinking for the acceptance of the post Kaliuga age,* then we should also be courageous enough to use his ideas literally.

Steiner's principles are to involve children in the concept of the whole and then place into that wholenesss the details, this an act of healing in the world today.

Furthermore we can open to all humans at all stages and ages all to the teachings of humanity. It is not a matter of: Do little ones understand? but: How can I put this subject into concepts on their level? – It was even Steiner who answered this to a teacher who was totally perplexed: . . . you can talk to the small children about any complex matter, but put it into a frame of love and choose the images which they are living in now. When later they again will hear about this and have a more mature grasp of it it is then built up upon the foundation of love and will be accepted with enthusiasm.

On this principle we are proposing to build a children's playground which consists of the five platonic solids and they will have the colours according to the knowledge which is

---

*In 1879 mankind as a whole stepped across the threshold and the archangel Michael took over the leading of mankind. In ages past the beings who took charge of universal guidance were Toth in the Egyptian culture, Hermes in Greek, Mercury Roman, and Michael in this age. They take up the energies and administer this for the sake of all Being.

Form, Sound, Colour and Healing

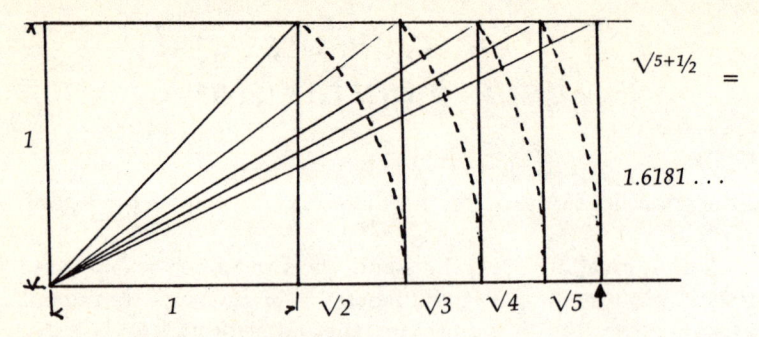

Fig. 5.1 The Golden mean (section).

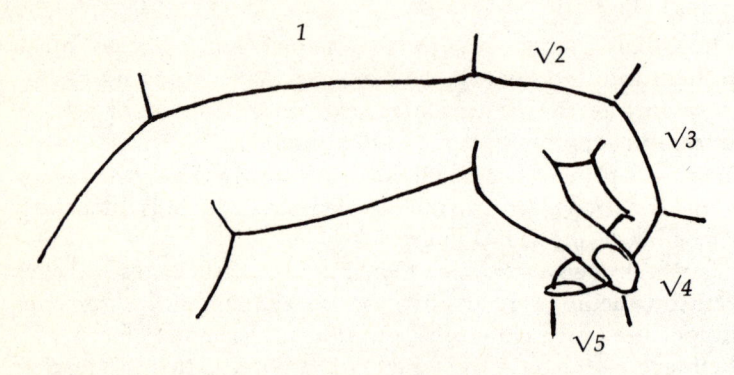

Fig. 5.2 The Golden Mean Concept Translated to the Human Anatomy.

handed down to us from the ancient Greek culture but re-examined with modern consciousness.

Using together with these forms 'cut outs' which are made to the Fibonacci measurements of golden mean (see illustration).

These five 'Wendy houses' standing in about an 18 × 12 metres area will be each approximately 2 metres high; made of fibre glass which has very high durability and stability. The sections can be put together and taken apart for transport.

Since all the astronomical and universal proportions are in some way or another related to the five platonic solids (we also find this law reflected in the geological structures of crystals, still further even right down to the molecular structures of crystallisation) is this not a good reason to use such mathematical, geometrical and indeed healing patterns? see Fig. 5.1 and 5.2.

A Threefold Approach to a Patient – Involved Therapy

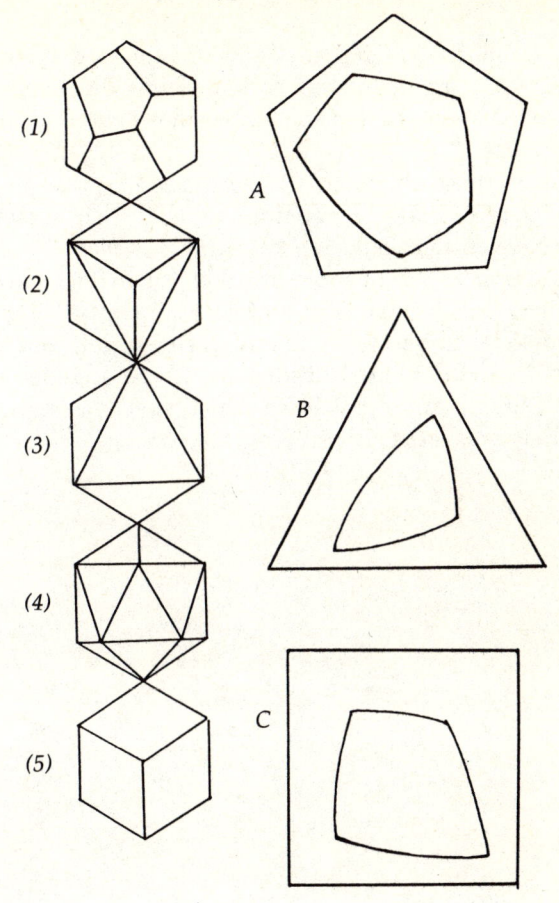

(1) Pentagondodecahedron — 108° angle of faces – violet colour
    Angel House — Harmony body, *touch* etc.
(2) Tetrahedron — 60° angle of faces – red colour
    Fire House — Fire body, *sight*
(3) Octahedron — 60° angle of faces – yellow colour
    Air House — Air body, *hearing*
(4) Icosahedron — 60° angle of faces – blue colour
    Water House — Water body, *smell*
(5) Hexahedron — 90° angle of faces – green colour
    Earth House — Earth (mineral) body, *taste*

Fig. 5.3 The Hexagonal Grid of the Platonic Solids 1–5 and the 'Cutouts' for Playground A–C.

Form, Sound, Colour and Healing

The kindergarten child will say: "I hide in the earth house." The sixth formers will go and measure the angles and the mathematical values and remember that they used to call it the earth house.

That all these five solids have indeed by way of form and colour very decisive therapeutic values for all ages of men, is made clear in the book: *Healing Through Colour.**

There is an inherent super or subconscious behaviour pattern built into each human soul, to find always in all circumstances the personal harmony to colour, form, sound and indeed all external, environmental influences. Given a choice eventually every one will go to that place which spells harmony with self and their present stage of being.

---

*Theo Gimbel 1980, Publishers C. W. Daniel

Bibliography of Reference Works used in Hygeia Research

Birren, Faber 1961: The Rational Approach to Colour in Hospitals.
Bjerke, André: Neue Beiträge zu Goethese Farbenlehre.
Bayes, Kenneth, FRIBA, FSIA: The Therapeutic Effect of Environment on Emotionally Disturbed and Mentally Subnormal Children.
Caligan, Joe: Research into Anti-glare illumination.
Chen, Li and Wang An-Sheng: Colour and 1966 Form Preferences in children; red, blue, green and yellow preferred in this order. Circle preferred by all.
Corinne, Heline "Colour & Music". New Age Press Inc., Box 372, Oceanside, Calif. 92054, U.S.A.
Davy, John. Science Editor, *The Observer Colour Magazine*.
Gimbel, Theo H: Healing Through Colour. C. W. Daniel, 1980.
Gimbel, Theo H. and Ashurst, P: An Investigation into Colour Concepts in Relation to Form, 1971.
Goethe, J. W. V.: Theory of Colour, 1810. Vol. 40, pp. 779 and 769.
Gregory, Richard Prof: Psychology Bristol University "Eye & Brain", World University Library, Weidenfeld & Nicolson, New Bond St, London, 1966.
Hanes, Randall M.: Diagnostic and Therapeutic Use of Colour. (Johns Hopkins University, Silver Springs, Md., U.S.A.)
IES Code for interior lighting. (pp. 19–24).
Kadinsky, Wassily, 1866–1944 Punkt & Linie zur Fläche Bauhaus-Bucher.
Keopfer, B., Ph.D and Kelly, D., M.D. Med. Sc.D.
Larson, C. Theodore (Coord 1955 (c)) Environmental Class-Study: The Effect of Windowless classrooms on small schoolchildren.

Majlath György Magyar Pszichological 1963 (preliminary pub.) Colour and Form as a Homogenial.

Neal, E: Visual Location of the Vertical, a built-in capacity not dependent on outer anchorage, 1926.

Ott, John, Dr. Health & Light, Published by Devin Edair Company, Old Greenwich, Con. U.S.A.

Proskauer, H. Q.: "Zum Studium von Goethes Farenlehre", Zbinden Verlag Basel, CH.

Rorschach, H. Psychodiagnostics, "The Rorschach Technique." a manual for a projective method of personality diagnosis.

Steiner Rudolf, Four lectures to Doctors 7th–9th Oct. 1920.

Steiner Rudolf, Colour Course: Die Schöpferische, Welt der. Farbe. "Dornach", Switzerland

Stirnimann F. "Uber das Farbempfinden Neugeborener" 1944.

Wilson, Michael and Brocklebank, Ralph, Colour-Hydro Tjerapy, Clent, Stourbridge, Worcs.